HOW TO BUILD YOUR OWN CASH FLOW EMPIRE.

ENJOYING MULTIPLE RESIDUAL AND PASSIVE INCOME STREAM

BY
OWEN LAWRENCE

Copyright © 2018 by Owen Lawrence. All rights reserved. No part of this publication may be reproduced or used in any manner whatsoever without the express written permission of the author or publisher except for the use of brief quotations in a book review. www.owenlawrence.site olaw2007@yahoo.com
Cover Design by Helen 20018 wealthgeniuspublisher@gemail.com

ISBN-13:
978-1718842366

ISBN-10:
1718842368

Disclaimer

Every effort has been made to accurately represent this product and its potential. Even though this industry is one of the few where one can write their own check in terms of earnings, there is no guarantee that you will earn any money using the techniques and ideas in these materials. Any claims made of actual earnings or examples of actual results can be verified upon request. Your level of success in attaining the results claimed in our materials depends on the time you devote to the program, ideas and techniques mentioned, your finances, knowledge and various skills. Since these factors differ according to individuals, we cannot guarantee your success or income level. Nor are we responsible for any of your actions.

DEDICATION

I want to dedicate this book to my family, to the manager of Owenroyalmultibusinesscompany and to all the members of my Microfinance team, I want to sincerely thank you all for the teamwork, the ideas and great work over the years. May God Almighty bless you and increase you. To all the investors Who believes in our ability to deliver.

TABLE OF CONTENTS

ACKNOWLEDGMENTS	7
DESCRIPTION AND INTRODUCTION	8
1 CHAPTER	11
How To Make Money With Your Writing	11
Types Of Writing	13
Where To Sell Your Writing	16
2 CHAPTER	24
HOW TO WRITE LEAD-PULLING SQUEEZE PAGES ON THE FLY	24
The Squeeze Page System	25
What You Need Before Getting Started on Your Squeeze Page	28
Planning Your Squeeze Page Theme	29
How to Write a Squeeze Page that Converts	31
Tips on Increasing Your Squeeze Page Conversion Rate	34
3 CHAPTER	38
How to Make a Lot Of Money Running WSO's	38

Where to Start	40
If you DON'T have any of these skills or products...	42
High Earning WSO Samples:	43
Sell Them The First Time Around	45
Most Profitable Niches and WSO's	46

4 CHAPTER — 52

Building The Business Brain — 52

Develop The Right Mindset To Transition From Employee To Entrepreneur	52
Perusing The Dream Synopsis	56
Possess a life outside your job.	57
Learn To Listen to Customers Synopsis	60
Find A Mentor And Coaching Synopsis	65

5 CHAPTER — 72

Build Your Own Cash Pipeline "Foolproof Strategies on How to Succeed in Network Marketing — 72

Network Marketer's Survival Guide	79
About Affiliate Marketing	87

6 CHAPTER — 89

The Expert Guide to Affiliate Marketing — 89

Super Affiliates Know Their Products	91

The 3 Things All Affiliate Marketers Need To Survive Online	94
So Many Affiliate Programs! Which One Do I Choose?	99
Why participate in an affiliate program?	102
Using Product Recommendations To Increase Your Bottom Line	107
Using Camtasia to Increase Your Affiliate Checks	110
For those who does not know it yet, how does Camtasia works?	111
How To Avoid The 3 Most Common Affiliate Mistakes	116
7 CHAPTER	**119**
iPhone & iPad App Cash	**119**
Generating App Ideas	119
Outsourcing Development	120
What Is Internet Marketing?	124

ACKNOWLEDGMENTS

First and foremost I want to acknowledge God almighty for his wisdom and strength up on my life, I also acknowledge the managing director. Mr. Adesotu Stanley Osagie, music films producer, Financial secretary Mrs. Judith Edosa, The number one investor mrs. Helen Lawrence Osagie and others, Wealthgeniuspublisher team , Thank you all so much, may God bless you and your families, May your going out and your coming in be blessed.

DESCRIPTION AND INTRODUCTION

DESCRIPTION

People will teach you, how to work for them, but they would not teach you how to work for yourself, I called that modern day slavery. I remember watching recently as a couple was being laid off from their long-term jobs. The wife said, with tears in her eyes, "For 18 years we worked hard for our security, and now we're out in the cold. It's not fair. She had only the illusion of security. She wasn't secure—she just thought she was.
Working for someone else, unless you own a piece of the profits, is not security. It's just the illusion of security. If you're going to become a home-based entrepreneur, you'd better learn which businesses have the potential for creating lifetime streams of income. This book will teach you how to set yourself and your family free by starting to build your own Cash flow Empire today. Your employer would not want you to know this so that you keep on working for them all the days of your life God forbid, out of 70 to 90% of the problem most people have, Is money problem or financial problem, you can almost do anything without money, but many of you have money that you did not know, if you have time you have money, because time is money, I started a micro Finance Company without having any money, but I have an idea and time, today the company loan money to people without having money, time and an idea is what I used. Whether the government create work or not in this book you will learn how to create multiple streams of income. The easiest way to set up residual and passive income streams! It's just that simple, it's the easiest and fastest way to do it and be financially free.

HOW TO BUILD YOUR OWN CASH FLOW EMPIRE. ENJOYING MULTIPLE RESIDUAL AND PASSIVE INCOME STREAM

INTRODUCTION

Among the hardest transitions for individuals is to move from the employee to the entrepreneur mentality. The idea of getting on your own, getting your own business is fantastic.

It's the desire of a lot of individuals to leave their jobs and get to be successful business owners.

However, is there a transition that has to be made from the employee mentality to the entrepreneur mentality?

It's really exceedingly crucial that you bear this entrepreneur mentality to succeed in business on your own…because most of the principles you'll need to succeed are based off of being a true entrepreneur.

And there are gigantic differences between that and an employee mentality, I'm not pulling your leg …and we will look at it here.

Many small business owners and enterprisers got their beginning as an employee. They worked for somebody else. The issue is, if you've been an employee for years, it may be difficult to shake of the bonds of the employee mentality.

What does this mean?

If you've an employee mentality, you're more likely to look to other people to tell you what to do. You'll find it difficult to take responsibility for the success and failure of your endeavor.

You see, as an employee, you've no say about how the business is executed. You just work hard to prove your value so that you can stay employed.

To read more of this go to Building The Business Brain

Residual Income Explained
Residual Income is another term for recurring income. In a nutshell, there are three (3) types of income streams that you may have coming into your business.
1. If you do a one-time job, sale or perform a contract, you get paid once and the income stops there.
2. If you do a normal 9 to 5 job, you will continue to get paid as long you continue to work for your employer—often called a linear income. This is the type of income that the majority of workers "enjoy." Even if you are a neurosurgeon, lawyer or engineer, you are only paid as long as you continue working. You stop working and the bank account dwindles.
3. The third type of income is the residual income where you are paid even after you have stopped working . For example, you wrote a book and as long as your book continues to sell, you will continue to receive royalty income for a work done once.
Majority of rich and affluent people created wealth through a form of residual income stream. Take Some singer for example; they still continues to receive royalty from the sales of their records made decades ago. They can even repackage the same oldies and sell them to generate new income. They don't have to spend time in the studio to record new songs in order to have the cash keep flowing in! This is the most ideal situation of the three. We would all like to work once and get paid over and over again. That is the power of recurring income.

1 CHAPTER

How To Make Money With Your Writing

If you're looking for a good way to earn some money on the internet - maybe even enough to quit your day job - one option is to provide writing services to other marketers. Even if you only consider yourself a half-decent writer, there are probably lots of opportunities out there for you to make some money.

As the saying goes, Content Is King, but not everybody is comfortable or even able to create that content. They are always looking for ways to create high- quality content for their websites, and one of the best ways to do that is by hiring a writer to create the content for them.

In this report we're going to look at some of the ways that you can earn money by writing, including some of the most effective places to find buyers for your work.

Let's get started.

Advantages Of Writing As A Business

There are several big advantages of getting into the "writing business."

• It's in demand • You can learn about the market(s) • You can find partners

First, writing is in demand. There are far more marketers who are looking for high quality content for their websites than there are writers providing it.

Sure, it's easy to find writers on sites like Elance or oDesk but if you've ever tried doing this yourself, you've probably experienced the lack of quality that many of those writers offer.

Some of them aren't native English speakers, others just have a poor work ethic - but the fact is, if you provide high-quality content and you're conscientious about the work you're doing, you will immediately distance yourself from 95% of your "competition."

Next, learning about the markets. I refer to this in the plural because you can learn a lot about internet marketing itself, as well as any markets that you write about.

If you provide high-quality content, and do so reliably, you will often be able to work with some successful - and maybe even well-known - marketers. They will often have you write on topics that they're involved in, and you can learn a lot by watching how they do things.

Believe me, the first time you write an ebook or report for someone and they take something they paid you $250 for and turn it into a $5,000 payday, it's going to open your eyes to the potential that's out there.

Along those same lines, you can often leverage these working relationships into further partnerships. Successful marketers understand that writing is often a stepping stone to bigger and better things. If you work with a marketer by writing for them, and later you graduate to creating and marketing your own products, that marketer is much more likely to partner up with you as an affiliate or JV (joint venture) partner because they know you and they know the quality of your work.

Types Of Writing

There are various types of writing that marketers are generally looking for. You can offer any or all of the following types of content:

• Articles • Blog posts • Reports • eBooks • Copywriting • Autoresponder emails • Spinning

Some of these are more specialized than others. Copywriting, for example, will require you to have a certain skill set that not all writers will have. Articles and blog posts, on the other hand, can generally be handled by virtually any writer (provided they are comfortable with the topic, of course).

.

These different levels of skill will also have a bearing on how much you can reasonably charge for your work. Article writers who are considered to be "highly paid" may charge $25 to $50 per article, somewhere around 500 words.

Highly paid copywriters, on the other hand, may earn $10,000 and up for a single sales letter, as well as a percentage of the sales in some cases.

If you're just starting out with your writing business, you're probably not going to be able to command those kind of rates until you've proven yourself, but it's something you can aspire to. Most writers who can command top-dollar for their work started out at entry-level rates, just like anyone else.

When you're first starting out, articles and blog posts are typically the easiest work to find. There are many places where you can market yourself as an article writer (which we'll cover in the next section) and there is a virtually never-ending supply of marketers and website owners who are looking for good content.

Reports and ebooks are also popular types of content for many writers. Both of these types of content are popular among internet marketers, and they are often looking for writers who can create them.

Reports and ebooks may be written to be sold, given away as bonuses for other products or even given away as incentive to get people to join email lists or other lead generation methods. Many marketers are constantly looking for new products or giveaways they can offer their customers, so from your point of view as a writer there is plenty of demand.

Writing reports and ebooks can be a good way to graduate into larger types of content and larger projects with your existing clients as well, so don't be afraid to offer your article clients larger projects.

We've already mentioned copywriting, and it tends to be one of the higher-paying forms of content, but in order to get paid well you need to have a proven track record. The first few sales letters you write may not generate the same kind of revenue, but if those sales letters convert well and you can build a bit of a portfolio of successful sales pages, it won't take long before you can start charging more.

HOW TO BUILD YOUR OWN CASH FLOW EMPIRE. ENJOYING MULTIPLE RESIDUAL AND PASSIVE INCOME STREAM

Autoresponder emails are another form of copywriting, in some ways, but they will vary depending on the ultimate purpose. Many marketers don't understand how to write effective emails, or they might not know enough about a particular niche to write them well, so by offering this type of content you can often land some fairly profitable clients.

Generally, marketers who are building niche email lists are working in more than one market. You may be able to get quite a bit of work by connecting with those marketers who need emails written for them.

Spinning is a bit of an unusual form of content, and not one that all writers are comfortable offering.

Article spinning is a bit of a controversial topic in the internet marketing world. Some people swear by it, while others feel it is a "black hat" technique that they would never use.

Spinning is basically the process of taking a base, or seed article and rewriting it with multiple versions of each sentence or even word replacements, using a particular format for those alternatives. Specialized software, called a "spinner" takes this "spun" article and outputs one or more unique versions.

The degree of uniqueness will be determined by how effectively the article is rewritten, and this is where a lot of marketers fail when using spun content. If you don't use enough replacements or you're not careful about the words you choose, you can wind up with a variation that isn't different enough from the original or worse, doesn't make sense.

If you offer article spinning as a service, you can make a pretty good profit per article - provided you're working with someone who understands the value you offer. It's not unheard of for people to pay $200 or more for a high-quality spun article. Even if it takes you four hours to create that single article, you can still earn a pretty good hourly wage this way.

Where To Sell Your Writing

There are several venues where you can sell your writing, some more profitable than others. The first one that you should always consider is your existing clients. If you're just starting out, this one may not work immediately, but once you've got a few jobs under your belt you should have a list of clients that you can go back to whenever you have time available to write.

Along those lines, always make sure you capture your customers' information - at least their name and email address - so you can contact them in the future. The fact is, they'll thank you for it - it's a win/win situation for both of you.

You'll have a list of people with whom you've already worked, and understand what they're looking for, and your customers will have a writer who they know they can trust to deliver high-quality content on time.

Before you go looking for new clients, always get in touch with your existing clients to see if they have any work for you.

HOW TO BUILD YOUR OWN CASH FLOW EMPIRE. ENJOYING MULTIPLE RESIDUAL AND PASSIVE INCOME STREAM

Another way your existing clients can help you generate more business is through referrals. You should always ask your clients for referrals, even if it's just a matter of letting them know that you're available if they know anyone who is looking for writing.

Marketers who need writing and don't have a writer they can trust will often turn to their friends and acquaintances in the internet marketing world for recommendations. If your clients are happy with your work, they will usually be willing to recommend you to those people.

In fact, you can even offer referral bonuses to really snowball your referrals. If you pay a "finder's fee" or offer a certain amount of free writing for every referral an existing customer sends you, this can really help to push the process along.

If you are looking for new customers, whether because you're just starting out or because your existing clients aren't looking for any new content at the moment, there are several effective places to turn.

One of the best places to find new clients is through forums. There are many different internet marketing forums, and many of them have sections where you can offer your services.

For example, if you've been involved in internet marketing for any length of time you're probably familiar with the Warrior Forum. There is a sub-forum on the site called Warriors for Hire where you can post an ad for your services. Or you could offer a special price on your writing services through the Warrior Special Offers section.

This is just one example, however - there are many other forums that have similar sections available to you.

There are a couple of caveats to forum marketing, however.

First, you need to take part in the forum and get to be known. If you rarely post or you join and immediately post an ad for your services, it's unlikely that you're going to find many clients.

People prefer to work with other people that they're familiar with. Even if you've never met them in person, you can get to "know" people through a forum. Post regularly and interact with other people to become known.

The other benefit you'll get from taking part regularly is that people will be able to see the quality of your writing from the posts you make on the forum. This can act as a sort of live portfolio of your work.

The second thing to be careful of when marketing on forums is choosing a forum that has a "cheap is better" mindset. Frankly, the Warrior Forum suffers from this problem in many ways. The WSO section has trained members of that forum to expect to pay rock-bottom prices for highly valuable products. This can translate across into other sections of the forum as well, such as Warriors For Hire.

That doesn't mean that you can't find high-paying clients on these forums, it's just a warning. You might get a better ROI by being active on other forums instead.

Another effective way to find new clients is through freelance websites like Elance.com and oDesk.com. These sites serve as a "middleman" connecting freelancers and people looking to hire those freelancers. They provide a certain amount of security for both parties, by moderating the jobs and acting as a sort of escrow service for the payments.

HOW TO BUILD YOUR OWN CASH FLOW EMPIRE. ENJOYING MULTIPLE RESIDUAL AND PASSIVE INCOME STREAM

The drawback, of course, is that they charge a fee for doing so. That fee is taken out of the service provider's payment (that's you) so you're essentially paying them to find new clients for you.

The most effective way to use these sites is to find new clients, and then once you have a bit of a working relationship with them you can move to working together directly. You might even offer a slightly lower rate since you don't have to pay the fee to the freelance sites.

For example, if you're paying them a 10% fee on every job you do, you could offer your client a 5% discount for working together directly and still wind up making more money.

Just be careful if you choose to pursue this option. Some of the freelance sites (such as [Fiverr.com](http://fiverr.com) for example) have rules about trying to move off site for future projects. You want to be sure that you're not breaking any rules by discussing this with your clients.

Another interesting way that you can sell your writing is by creating PLR, or Private Label Rights offers.

Private Label Rights means that the buyers have the right to use the content virtually any way they like. They can edit it however they wish, put their own name on it and generally treat it just like content they had written themselves.

The disadvantage of PLR from a buyer's perspective is actually one of its strongest advantages from the seller's (yours):

Multiple people can buy the rights to the same content

From the buyer's perspective, this means that there are other people who can use the same content - sell it, use it as web content, give it away, etc. Which creates a certain amount of competition compared to having exclusive rights to the content.

But from your perspective, as the seller, you can sell the same content many times over. This means you can charge less for it and still wind up making more money.

For example, let's say you've written ten 500-word articles. If you were to sell those to a single client, and charged them $20 per article (4 cents per word) you would earn $200. If you took those same ten articles and sold them as a PLR bundle charging only $10 for the entire pack ($1 per article) you would only need to sell 20 copies to make the same amount of money.

It highly likely that you could find more than 20 buyers if the articles were on a popular topic, and the quality is good. In fact, you might sell 100 copies or more, generating much more revenue with exactly the same amount of work.

There is another benefit to selling PLR content, however - you get your writing in front of a lot more people, some of whom might be looking for exclusive content as well. If they see your PLR articles are well-written it's quite likely that they would be interested in working with you for exclusive projects as well.

Think of selling PLR as a "front end" offer, with your writing services as the back end "upsell."

How Much Should You Charge?

The big question on many writers' minds, especially when they're just getting started, is how much to charge for their work. This is a tough thing for many people to decide. After all, they want to earn as much as possible and they may feel that their work is worth a lot. But until they've had a chance to prove themselves, buyers may not want to pay high-end rates.

Typically, the best way to charge for your writing is on a per-word basis. You could charge 1 cent, 2 cents, 5 cents or more per word:

- 1 cent per word = $5 per 500 word article • 2 cents per word = $10 per 500 word article • 5 cents per word = $25 per 500 word article • etc.

The same calculations would be used for longer types of content. For example, a 2,500 word report would cost $125 at 5 cents per word.

There are a couple of things you'll need to consider when setting your prices. The first is what sort of competition do you have? One of the forums I frequent has a "Writers for Hire" section where most of the writers charge 1 cent per word. If you were to post an offer there at 5 cents per word, chances are you wouldn't get many takers.

The other thing to consider is whether or not people are familiar with your skills and the quality of your work. If not, you may need to start at a lower price in order to get some experience and to prove yourself to your potential clients.

A good strategy in this case is to make an "introductory" offer at a lower price than you normally charge, and make that clear in the offer itself. Let people know that it's a special offer and any future work will be at your regular rates.

You'll most likely get some buyers who only sign up because of the discount, but you'll also probably get some buyers who continue to work with you at your regular rates once they've seen the quality of your work.

This type of offer can be a good way to get some more clients into your "funnel" whenever you feel the need to find new ones. As your writing business expands, you'll soon find that you can only work with a maximum number of people at any given time. Ideally, you want to have a few more regular clients than you can handle all at once. By doing this, you can often keep your writing schedule filled without any need to find new business.

Specializing

The last strategy we'll discuss in this report is specializing in a certain niche or certain topics. If you are an expert in a particular market, you might want to consider writing exclusively for that market - especially if it's a profitable one. For example, you might specialize in fitness and weight loss topics exclusively.

There are a couple of advantages to this strategy:

1. It's easier to write about topics you're familiar with 2. You can charge more because you're an expert

If you pick a topic you know well, it can make the writing process much faster since you won't need to do as much research. And the quality of your writing will generally be a lot better than if you're writing about topics that you're only superficially familiar with, from doing some basic research.

And because your writing will generally be much higher quality, you can charge more for it. Your customers will be getting true expert content, so they will often be happy to pay you the higher prices.

Even with all the automation tools that are out there for building websites and populating them with content, there is always going to be a market for high-quality writing. If you enjoy writing, and can provide that high-quality to your clients, you'll have a virtually never-ending market for your skills.

And getting started is the hardest part. Once you've got a bit of experience under your belt and have some happy clients, you can leverage that into a full-time writing business if that's your ultimate goal.

Remember - the internet revolves around content. That's unlikely to change anytime soon, so if you can help other marketers by providing the content that they need, your services are going to be in demand for a long time to come.

2 CHAPTER

HOW TO WRITE LEAD-PULLING SQUEEZE PAGES ON THE FLY

Before you begin the attempt to build a successful list or create a powerful sales page, you will want to start with a rigorous introduction to Squeeze Pages.

In stark contrast to undifferentiated, unfocused home pages, Squeeze Pages focus specifically on capturing leads for a newsletter or making sales for a specific product – and make no attempt to give visitors a different option.

Another common word that is often used to describe Squeeze Page, is "squeeze page" (or "lead capture page" in some circles). A squeeze page is a page designed to get names and email addresses. Usually, however, a squeeze page is usually a smaller type of Squeeze Page, which usually has an opt-in form in sight when the page loads.

So what is important to learn in an introduction to Squeeze Pages? First, it is important to recognize that all successful marketers use these. If you plan to sell a product over the Internet, you will want to use one, too, rather than relying on sidebar opt-in forms and unfocused pages that do not convey a single point and a single call to action.

Another important thing you will want to take away from this introduction to Squeeze Pages is that every Squeeze Page contains the same parts and is focused on a SINGLE goal – getting the visitor to become a subscriber or buyer.

HOW TO BUILD YOUR OWN CASH FLOW EMPIRE. ENJOYING MULTIPLE RESIDUAL AND PASSIVE INCOME STREAM

These parts are as follows: an opt-in form (or sales prompt), a brief or lengthy introduction, a picture of the list/product owner, the signature of the list owner, and a call to action (or multiple calls to action).

Determining which model will work best for you can simply only be done through testing. While many boast a conversion and attribute it to the shortness of their introduction

(many will be one short paragraph), otherwise will boast a high conversion rate because they use lengthy, thorough, and compelling copy.

If there is anything you absolutely must take away from an introduction to Squeeze Pages, it is that you cannot create a Squeeze Page or squeeze page that isn't focused.

The Squeeze Page System

The Squeeze Page system provides a uniquely powerful system through which you can derive profit from multiple streams. This article will briefly discusses some of those different streams – and how you can manipulate them.

Let's start with the Squeeze Page itself: all traffic is sent to the Squeeze Page. From there, it will have a number of options, depending on what you have given them. Many marketers suggest that your Squeeze Page should always be an opt-in form. Others will suggest that it should simply be a sales page.

Whether it's a free newsletter or a product for sale, the Squeeze Page system you create should include a "one time offer," which will compel them to take action – subscribe, buy, etc.

Once they subscribe or buy, the Squeeze Page system you create should then re-route them to a thank you page, which opens up more means through which you can up-sell. One quick way to up-sell is to simply include advertisements on your thank you page for related affiliate products or for your own products. Here, again, you will want to give them a one-time offer.

Also, if you haven't yet asked them to join your mailing list, this is where you should do it – on your thank you page. Once they opt-in to your list, you now have a whole new option you can use in conjunction with the Squeeze Page system to generate revenue.

One such option is selling ad space in your newsletter or e-zine. The more people you have reading your newsletter, the more you can generally charge for ad space; however, you will want to avoid overselling to your list to ensure your advertisers actually make money.

Your next option is to endorse a product as an affiliate. You can tell your subscribers how someone has just created a brilliant product – and you can offer it to your subscribers through an affiliate link. You may even want to use other products you have has bonuses to give them something extra.

The last and most profitable way in which you can generate revenue through your newsletter is by creating and selling your own products to them.

HOW TO BUILD YOUR OWN CASH FLOW EMPIRE. ENJOYING MULTIPLE RESIDUAL AND PASSIVE INCOME STREAM

It is important to note that you don't have to use all of these means to generate revenue; however, the more you use, the more you earn in general.

Your Squeeze Page
Your One Time Offer (OTO)

Thank You Page

Back-end Ads & Selling

Sell Ad Space in Your eZine

Subscription to your Mailing List

Endorse as an Affiliate

Sell your own product

What You Need Before Getting Started on Your Squeeze Page

Before you get started building your Squeeze Page, you will need a number of things to a) make your offer actually have a point; and b) facilitate the creation of your Squeeze Page.

One thing you absolutely must have before you get started is an auto responder. Without any auto responder, you are tossing potential bags of money in the garbage. Rather than creating a relationship with customers and potential customers – and giving yourself the opportunity to attempt future up-sales -- you're allowing them to leave and never return.

In addition to an auto responder, you will need to have an actual offer that people want to buy. You may want to develop a product, such as an E-Book or a piece of software.

If you don't have the skills to do either, you can always hire a professional to do it for you through Elance.com or Guru.com. You will then either want to sell this product and attempt to get subscribers from your thank you page – or you will want to get subscribers by offering the product for free (which is what many Internet marketers now do).

Another thing you absolutely must have before you get started is a check out service. You may want to consider Paypal, Clickbank, or 2 Check Out. All of these services will allow you to make transactions quickly.

Another thing you must have before you get started is a set of graphics, which usually includes a graphic header, a check out button, background wallpaper, and a half-decent picture of yourself. You can probably provide the picture of yourself, but you might want to hire a professional to do the rest.

Another thing you will need before you can get started on your Squeeze Page is some way in which to create a realistic signature. http://www.vletter.com is probably your best bet; but, if you're on a budget, you may want to opt for simply using a word processing program.

Planning Your Squeeze Page Theme

Perhaps the most important part of creating a Squeeze Page is planning your Squeeze Page theme. How you select your theme, of course, will all depend on how you plan to generate traffic.

If you decide to generate traffic through search engine optimization, planning your Squeeze Page theme will entail finding phrases within your niche which have a high demand (aggregate search value) and a low supply (small amount of competing sites) and then creating multiple Squeeze Pages, each which is optimized around a different phrase.

If, on the other hand, you decide to generate traffic through pay per click (PPC) programs, such as Adwords, planning your Squeeze Page theme will again entail tuning a number of different pages to fit the keywords you are purchasing.

This is actually where most people fail when they create a Squeeze Page: they don't tune it to fit a specific audience. For instance, in the case of a squeeze page for a newsletter, they might start a newsletter about toys, but they only create one Squeeze Page and send all traffic to it. This is a big mistake.

Chances are, if you create a quality product or newsletter, it can benefit a number of people. So why not communicate the exact benefits they will derive from subscribing or buying?

If, for instance, you have a newsletter about Legos and toy blocks, so you group it under the loose heading of "toys," a visitor who is looking specifically for information about either Legos or toy blocks will click off your page if they don't see the direct connection to the exact topic for which they were searching.

Instead, you will want to setup a page centered around Legos and a page centered around toy blocks. On each page, you will want to communicate the specific benefits to joining the list for each of those groups of visitors.

Going one step further, in addition to planning your Squeeze Page theme, if you are creating a Squeeze Page for a newsletter, you may also want to segment your list, so you can send information specifically about Legos to those who request it – and information about blocks to those who request it.

How to Write a Squeeze Page that Converts

Most people have no (or simply the slightest) idea how to write a Squeeze Page that converts. Instead, they slop together elements that they have seen used in other Squeeze Pages – but usually do not put them together in the same way the owner of the successful Squeeze Page did.

One major problem is copy. And that's fine. Not everyone is going to be an excellent writer – never mind a copywriter. But as someone selling a product or trying to build a list, it is important that you know your strengths and weaknesses – and that you either spend the time to overcome them or hire someone else to do it for you.

With copywriting, for instance, it is important to use a mix of compelling sales points with powerful psychological triggers. Most people who create a sales page miss either one or both of those elements.

For instance, they might concentrate so much on building hype that they don't actually explain what solution they are providing – and for whom they are providing it. If I don't have a specific problem that your product solves, why would I buy it? I wouldn't.

Now, if they fail to sprinkle in psychological triggers, such as "scientifically proven," "guaranteed," and "shocking," no one will feel compelled to continue reading, as the benefits will have a low or average perceived value.

In addition to these two problems, some sales pages lack coherency and direction. The copy looks amateurish and it doesn't slowly grind forward, breaking down the visitor's resistance to the sale – and compelling him or her to buy more and more at each sales point.

Additionally, if there aren't multiple calls to action – another form of psychological trigger – then a potential visitor might never feel compelled enough to pull out his or her credit card on the spot and make the purchase.

In addition to careful copywriting, there are other important things you must take into consideration when writing a Squeeze Page that converts. For instance, it is important to build a compelling case for a time-bound offer.

Now, this doesn't mean you have to invent fake deadlines and constantly revise them each week. This is a good way to guarantee your complete loss of credibility in the shortest amount of time possible.

However, when planning your copy, you will want to make sure that you constantly urge the reader to act immediately by inserting a number of "calls to action," as I've mentioned previously.

You may want to consider using fly-ins or pop-ups to create more urgency – or to make a time-bound offer. Perhaps you can use a countdown to build urgency (i.e., when someone arrives at your Squeeze Page, they have five minutes to purchase the product at the lowest price).

Now, if you're creating a squeeze page, you might want to employ slightly different tactics. Rather than building a compelling case with multiple triggers and calls to action over the course of 1000 words, you may want to simply condense that all into a compelling headline and one paragraph of "benefits."

For a completely free-to-join squeeze page, you more than likely won't have a considerable amount of resistance to joining, unless the visitor: a) Doesn't see any benefits; and b) Suspects that you will sell their email address to spammers.

Both of these problems are relatively easy to overcome. In your headline, simply state the exact benefits they will receive for joining – as always, mixing in psychological triggers.

In your first paragraph of copy, give them a compelling reason to join now (i.e., the price might go up, the list might become private, you'll get this amazing report).

Now, to overcome the second problems, simply include a short line under your opt-in form that explains that you will not – under any circumstances – spam them or sell or give away their email address and name.

Tips on Increasing Your Squeeze Page Conversion Rate

There are three major ways in which you can create your Squeeze Page conversion rate. All Squeeze Pages created by professionals usually include these three elements at a few others.

The first way in which you can increase your conversion rate is through personalization. This is usually done in two ways: the first way is by providing a photo of yourself. The second way is by adding your signature to the bottom of your Squeeze Page.

This radically increases visitors' trust. Most people who resist buying products online do so because they're weary of getting scammed by a faceless liar, who won't be around when they need help or when they need to return the product.

Tip: By adding your picture and signature, you can significantly increase a gain in your visitors' trust. ☺

Another way in which you can increase your Squeeze Page conversion rate is by using black text or a white layout. Regardless of what anyone tells you, this is one of the easiest ways in which to make your page look professional, rather than pathetic or desperate.

The third way in which you can gain trust is by offering something for free. This is generally what you will do if you're using a squeeze page to generate leads: you'll offer a free report or five-day course – and then use that to generate leads, which you will later upsell or generate revenue from via affiliate sales. Why is this technique so effective?

Quite simply because it allows them to judge your work and ideas before they actually have to pay for them. Additionally, it builds trust.

In addition to these three general ways in which to increase your conversion rate, you should always guarantee a product. If you sell through Clickbank, you actually don't have a choice.

But if you're using Paypal or some other check out (Credit Card processing) program, you will want to make sure you clearly state that customers can return your product for any reason within a given period of time after the purchase.

Follow all of these steps and you will significantly increase your Squeeze Page conversion rate.

Driving Targeted Traffic into Your Squeeze Page

Driving traffic into your Squeeze Page – it sounds easy, doesn't it? Well, it's not. And no matter how great your Squeeze Page is, it won't matter if no one ever reads it.

Furthermore, if everyone in the world other than your target audience reads it, it also won't matter. This is why you need to find media through which you can drive targeted visitors to your Squeeze Page.

One way in which you can drive traffic to your Squeeze Page is through natural search engine optimization. This is the slowest process, but it is also one of the best ways to ensure a continually increasing stream of traffic over time.

Generating natural search engine traffic generally entails getting links to your site. While reciprocal linking was once the best strategy, experts now believe that major search engines are devaluing reciprocal links in favor of one-way links and triangular links (which search engines can't really detect).

Another way in which to get natural search engine traffic is by optimization your website for certain key phrases. You can do this by creating pages that specifically focus on one keyword on your given niche. You can then set the page extension to that keyword and optimize the content at a 1.5% density for that keyword. You will also want to use it in header and title tags.

Now, in addition building natural search engine traffic, you will want to consider using pay per click advertising. You can do this by opening an account with Google Adwords.

As mentioned earlier, successful Google Adwords campaigns do two things: they group keywords into multiple, small, related groups – and they send leads to multiple, tweaked Squeeze Pages.

This means you will have to start with some careful keyword research; and you will then have to alter your Squeeze Pages to match that research. These are some of the most commonly used tools for driving traffic to a Squeeze Page; however, they are not always the most effective.

Now, both of those methods can be effective, but they both usually have rather high barriers to entry and require a lot of work.

HOW TO BUILD YOUR OWN CASH FLOW EMPIRE. ENJOYING MULTIPLE RESIDUAL AND PASSIVE INCOME STREAM

Luckily, you do have another option: human connections. And this is where most Internet marketers fail. They don't realize the power of human connections because they are so caught up in the idea of making transactions and collecting massive checks without having to deal with customers and clients.

One quick way to get traffic through human connections is a joint venture. You can enter into a joint venture by compiling a list of possible "partners" -- or people who might be able to assist you in some mutually-beneficial way. This list might include other list owners in your niche, site owners in your niche, and experts.

There's only one important thing you should keep in mind when contacting joint venture partners – and that is to make it as quick, easy, and beneficial for them as possible. If they have no incentive for doing it, they probably won't even reply to you. And if it isn't easy, they'll accept other joint venture offers over yours.

Another way in which you can drive traffic to your Squeeze Page is through blog and forum posting; however, it is important that you do not spam, as many businesses do.

Instead, actually participate on the forum, provide people with something of value; and, after a while, post your product in your signature – and try to network with people on the forum who work in similar fields.

Your approach to blog posting should be similar. Include a signature file that links back to your Squeeze Page, but don't spam. Instead, post useful comments. This is not only more ethical, but it is plainly more effective. Spam gets deleted. Good comments get praised, inducing people to follow your link and check out your products.

3 CHAPTER

How to Make a Lot Of Money Running WSO's

By a Warrior Who Has Earned Over $15,000 from the WSO Forum Alone in the Last 5 Months

About the WSO Forum

The WSO Forum (Warrior SPECIAL OFFERS Forum) is designed to allow warriors to offer other warriors (ONLY) quality products and/or services at a special discounted price. The offer cannot be given anywhere else at the same price. If the product and/or service is to be offered elsewhere, it must be at a higher price, that is the rule. It also must be an original work/product/service of your own and can NOT be a PLR product, even if you change it.

It can however, be a product that someone creates for you and ONLY you. No one else can have the product to sell or the PLR or resale rights but you. This would be just like outsourcing somebody to make a product for you and only you. Then you may sell it as a WSO.

HOW TO BUILD YOUR OWN CASH FLOW EMPIRE. ENJOYING MULTIPLE RESIDUAL AND PASSIVE INCOME STREAM

For example, if you have a web designer build you a template that has an easy to use admin area where anybody could enter their Google AdSense ID and other affiliate ID's and have their own money making site in whatever niche they want...you can make sure that you have the exclusive rights to it, and then sell it as a WSO at a great WARRIOR ONLY SPECIAL PRICE. This is just one example of many that I will cover in this report.

The WSO forum is an extremely generous gift of Allen Says, the owner of the Warrior Forum; it is a perfect example of the spirit of the forum and the generosity and kindness of true warriors. People truly have launched $30,000 a month businesses from the WSO forum alone and continue to do so today.

I personally have earned over $15,000 from the WSO forum alone in the five months that I have been running them. I average a $3,000-$4,000 a month business JUST FROM WSO's and it continues to grow. For that I am extremely thankful and since I am a teacher at heart, I want to share as much wisdom with you as I can.

Again, the WSO forum is truly a gift and should not be taken for granted.

Where to Start

If you don't have a particular product or service to offer, let's think of what you can do. But first, let's actually go over what products and services are the most popular on the WSO forum.

Services:

- Article and/or Ghostwriting Services

- Copywriting Services

- Web Design

- Graphic Design

- Ad Campaign Services

- SEO

- Software Development

- Programming

- Wordpress Blog Building

- Social Marketing

- Coaching/Mentoring

- More...

Products:

- E-Books or Reports with PLR and RR/MRR

- E-Books that will be helpful to marketers

- Software that helps solve IM problems

- Software with PLR or MRR or RR

- Templates

- Marketing Techniques

- Pre-Built Businesses/Websites

- Business Plans or Business Models

- E-Courses

- Newsletters

- Membership Subscriptions

- New Marketing Methods

- More...

If you DON'T have any of these skills or products...

Think like a Millionaire!

...You can easily hire people to do some (or all) of it for you. If you want to run an article writing WSO but you can't write well, gather up a team of people or just one person who you can pay to write articles for you. Negotiate a percentage split, something like 50/50 or 60/40 (you get 40% because they are writing). Of course, your reputation is on the line so you must make sure they write quality articles and can handle the orders. Then, you can run your WSO; the money will come in, you will pay your writer(s) and then deliver the finished work to the client.

If you charge $5 per article and sell them in let's say packs of 5 for $25, you will make $12.50 for every order that comes in and all you had to do was find a writer and pay $20 for posting the WSO.

This same technique can be applied to ALL the above mentioned services and products. There is Elance.com and Rentacoder.com where you can also find talented people who do great work for very low prices.

You can get help writing an entire ebook or report from someone who is good at writing. You can hire a graphic designer to design a bunch of really cool looking 'buy now' buttons and sell it as a graphics package on the WO forum. The list goes on and on but you must always think like a millionaire. What can you do to make money next? You KNOW what works, you see the popular WSO's....why aren't you grabbing a piece of the action?!

This is how multi-million dollar businesses are run. They outsource most of the work to people who are BETTER than they are at it. That is the 'Millionaire' mindset that you have to maintain. People are going to be better than you at web design, at writing, etc. so why not hire them instead of compete with them? That is precisely how Bill Gates built his empire.

If you DO have any of the above skills or products...

...Well now it's time to gather a few reviews and testimonials from fellow warriors. Offer your services and/or products free or cheap to members in exchange for an honest review or testimonial. Get some feedback and reviews and maybe make some tweaks/adjustments to your product based on the feedback.

Writing Your WSO Sales Copy

When attacking this beast, you must remember that warriors are sometimes skeptical of products/services, especially if they are "over hyped" up. If you write your own sales copy, try not to be so full of yourself and your offer. Using superlatives like "Amazing, Super, Marvelous, Fantastic, Unbelievable, Etc." will probably not work that well on the WSO forum, maybe somewhere else it would.

High Earning WSO Samples:

Here is a link to a WSO of mine that generated over $5,000 in sales:

http://www.warriorforum.com/forum/topic.asp?TOPIC_ID=244058

Here is a link to another WSO of mine that has also generated over $5,000 in sales:

http://www.warriorforum.com/warrior-special-offers-forum/801-9733-plr-10-000-200-000-visitors-60-days-9733-a.html

---

Here is a firesale that I just ran as a WSO this month (Aug 2008) and it has raked in great cash so far in just a few days!

http://www.warriorforum.com/warrior-special-offers-forum/1055-9733-plr-poduct-firesale-limited-only-5-9733-a.html

---

WSO Forum Etiquette

Use these as an example for how people like to be talked to and treated. Customer service is so important; if you fail in that department I don't know if you'll make it very far.

It is not polite to run a WSO and then 'disappear' and go to a movie with your girlfriend or boyfriend! This is perhaps the biggest pet peeve of WSO frequenters. They think to themselves (rightfully so...), "Why on earth would so-and-so run a WSO and then not be around to answer my questions?" or to send them their download link? Sometimes people have questions and they'll post them on the WSO itself.

If you are not around to answer that question, people will actually wait to buy your product until you answer. Either because they have the same question themself or because they want to see if you are reputable and reliable. If you take two days to answer someone's question, you will most definitely lose business.

Don't get angry with your customers either or have an attitude. This will hurt your WSO. The CUSTOMER IS ALWAYS RIGHT!

I have abided by that law no matter how hard I've had to bite my tongue in the past and it has brought me nothing but great success.

Sell Them The First Time Around

You want to get people interested enough to buy your WSO after seeing it the FIRST time! Otherwise, they may never get around to finding it again...

5 Tips on how to do this:

1. OVER-DELIVER and don't be afraid to let people know that you are over-delivering! Give a bonus away for free or better yet, lower your price even a little bit more and tell everyone you did so. This will make it easier for the buyer to make the decision to purchase your WSO.

2. Make sure that your WSO Headline and offer are congruent with each other. If your headline sounds really awesome, but your product or sales pitch doesn't live up...you will see a lot of views, but poor conversions. The more honest you are in your headline and copy, the more REAL customers you will obtain and the less refund requests you will have.

3. Offer refunds and guarantees! This will boost your sales and conversions considerably. Tell them if they are unsatisfied for any reason, they can have a full refund, no questions asked. You can even put a 30 day time limit on refund requests if you desire. There are some people who will ask for refunds but the amount of sales you will get from offering the guarantee, will outweigh the refunds for sure! Trust me.

4. Be straight and to the point. Nobody wants to hear your life story! Make a nice red headline, bold and centered at the top. Write a short but sweet sales copy including everything we've discussed and more and then an easy to access payment link.

5. I recommend using a payment link that goes right to a payment processor where they can type in their credit card info or use PayPal right then and there. If you take them to another sales page, you will lose a lot of potential purchases, that's just the way it is. As you saw when you purchases THIS report, I had a PayPal button on a simple HTML page and nothing else. Simple, easy and NO other option but to pay.

Most Profitable Niches and WSO's

In my opinion, the best type of WSO to run right now is one that offers a specific service such as article marketing and/or press release writing. Also, social marketing and blog posts fall into this same category.

Next would be a product of your own. I am good at teaching music so I wrote several books that teach people how to play guitar and other instruments. I sold these as a WSO to other marketers (instead of people who want to learn guitar) so that they can turn around and sell them to people who want to learn guitar. I sold the PLR and RR to them. (Private label rights and Resale Rights). They can change it, leave it the same, put their name on it, resell it, give it away to build their list, etc, etc.

HOW TO BUILD YOUR OWN CASH FLOW EMPIRE. ENJOYING MULTIPLE RESIDUAL AND PASSIVE INCOME STREAM

Try to write a report or e-book about something that you are knowledgeable about, or again, OUTSOURCE the writing. It can be done very inexpensively and the money you can make from the WSO will far surpass the investment of getting some help.

These niches are the most popular right now:

- Weight Loss
- Fitness
- Make Money Online
- Domain Flipping
- Dog Training
- Water4Gas
- DNA Personalized Nutrition
- GPS
- iPhones
- Blogging
- Video
- Online Gambling
- Design
- Web Traffic
- SEO
- Marketing Techniques
- Article Marketing (Bum Marketing)
- PLR and MRR

If you can come up with a quality report, e-book or service that revolves around one of the above mentioned niches, you will have no problem making a lot of money on the WSO forum.

If you write ten articles on something you know about (or do a few hours of research about), let's say you write 10 water4gas review articles. You can charge $5 for the PLR to all 10 water4gas articles. That comes out to only .50 cents per article, which you would mention in your sales copy of course. If you sell 50 of them, you just made yourself $250. You invested $20 in the WSO and it took you maybe 10 hours or less worth of work. Even at 10 hours worth of work that comes out to $25 an hour, not bad if you ask me! With hundreds of warriors being on the forum at ALL times, selling 50 of those '10-packs' wouldn't be hard at all.

Build Relationships

When you run a WSO, your buyers may very well end up being buyers for life. Follow up with them after you make the sale and see if they would be interested in hearing about future offers of yours. Since they bought from you, you are legally allowed to send them emails unsolicited for up to two years I believe. Next WSO you run, send out an email to all of your previous buyers...you may just get surge of purchases before your WSO even gets attention from forum surfers.

I have built lifelong business relationships on the warrior forum and most all of them were because of the WSO forum in one way or another.

Extras:

HTML Trick for WSO Forum

A neat trick is to use HTML code in the title/headline of your WSO ad. If you type &#9733 YOURTITLEHERE, after posting it, you will see a star, followed by the title. These ASCII codes are used all the time on the WSO forum and it helps attract attention to your WSO even when it's down further on the page. You can make hundreds of different symbols by typing the &# symbols followed by four or five digit numbers. As I said before, &#9733 makes a star. &#9835 makes a cool looking music note. You can Google HTML symbols and find lists of all different cool ones. This gives your WSO a better chance at being seen, AND it impresses the reader because you know how to put 'code' onto your title.

The Low Price Idea Theory

I have ran many WSO's and the ones that earned me the most money and had the least amount of refunds, were the one's priced the lowest. I have made more money off of one WSO that I sell for $4 than I have from another one that sold for $12! People love good prices and that is what the WF and WSO forum are all about! Sharing your knowledge and being generous. Why not over-deliver?
I am working on a WSO that is going to be packed full of value, but only will cost $1 or $2 dollars. I figure...so many people will order it and NO ONE will ask for a refund.

ADDING A PAYMENT LINK TO YOUR WSO!

This part is easy, but a lot of people requested this information...so here it is!

To add a "Click Here to Buy My WSO Now" link to your WSO, that takes your customer to your PayPal payment page where they can pay you with their PayPal account or a credit card, you must first log in to your PayPal account.

Then, you will click on the tab that says "Merchant Services."

Once you've clicked on the 'Merchant Services' tab, you will see an icon that says "Buy Now Button" and you want to click on that.

Inside the "Buy Now Button" you can enter the name of your product (or service) as well as the price you wish to charge. If it's a $7 report, or a $2,000 service it doesn't matter, you can type it in the box that says 'price'.

Then, all you have to do is click "Create Button!" and that's it! You will be directed to a page that gives you the HTML code for your custom payment button. There will be TWO TABS on this section...one that says "Website" and one that says "Email."

To add a nice looking, shiny yellow "Buy Now" button to your website, you'll want to copy and paste the HTML code from the "Website" Tab.

However, if you want to add a TEXT PAYMENT LINK to your WSO, you will simply click on the "Email" tab. This will give you a shorter line of code, which is just a URL, that you can copy and paste into your WSO sales copy. When someone clicks on the link, it will take them to the PayPal payment page, just as it did when you bought this very report from me.

You can get even more advanced and have the customer sent to a specific URL after they have made a SUCCESSFUL payment. This means that you can offer INSTANT DOWNLOADS for your Products that you sell on the WSO Forum!!! This gives you a tremendous advantage over others, because many people want to have instant delivery of their product and you can get many more buyers by offering this.

To do it, you must click on "Advanced Options" before you click the "Create Button" link. This would be after you type in the product/service name and the price.

In the advanced options section, you can enter a URL (Web address) that every customer will be taken to after successful payment has been made. You can also enter a URL for when their payment is denied if you wish.
On the page that you send them to after successful payment...you would have your product on that page with a download link to the product. You would have to design this page yourself, or you could use a template.

HOW TO BUILD YOUR OWN CASH FLOW EMPIRE. ENJOYING MULTIPLE RESIDUAL AND PASSIVE INCOME STREAM

That's how you add a text PayPal payment link to your WSO!...pretty easy right?

I hope you have been inspired to get going with your WSO. Taking action, as everyone always says, is really the best thing you can do. Hey, If you don't make a lot of money from your first WSO, you will certainly know what to do better or differently the next time, right?

The WSO forum is a place to get hundreds of targeted visitors to your ad daily and if you follow the above advice and perspectives, I can't see you failing. You must find a demand for something, and then fill it. If every warrior is talking about video marketing and video this and that....you might want to consider a WSO that is related to video. Heck, you could even make a video about how to make a video! That would be a great seller on the WSO board.

Beat Everyone Else's Price

If you beat everyone else's price, you will come out a winner. If the going rate for articles or a video about 'how to make a video' is $XX amount of money, charge a little bit less. If 5 articles normally costs people $25-35, do it for $20 and you'll get the business!

If there's a newbie ebook that sells for $12, sell yours for $9 or $10...get it? This method has worked wonders for me!

Now go back up to the links I gave you to study some of my most successful WSO's.

I wish you all the best of luck and success with your WSO endeavors

4 CHAPTER

Building The Business Brain

Develop The Right Mindset To Transition From Employee To Entrepreneur

Which One Are You?

If you're an entrepreneur or business owner, you think much differently. Essentially the buck stops (and begins) with you. You're responsible for the success and failure of your endeavor. And you are the one who makes all the huge decisions (including who to designate littler decisions to!).

HOW TO BUILD YOUR OWN CASH FLOW EMPIRE. ENJOYING MULTIPLE RESIDUAL AND PASSIVE INCOME STREAM

To discover if you're thinking like an employee or an entrepreneur, take this fast quiz:

• Do you confine your tasks/responsibilities to a subset of what is required for your business to flourish? • Do you base your life-style on your revenue? • If a money setback happens, do you shrink your budget to adapt to the reduction in revenue? • Do you constantly seek outside advice to make even daily decisions?

If you responded "yes" to most of these queries, chances are you've an employee mentality. Here's why those with an entrepreneur mentality would answer "no."

Do you confine your tasks/responsibilities to a subset of what is required for your business to flourish?

Entrepreneurs understand that occasionally they have to do things in their business that are "higher up" or "beneath" their skill level. Their mental attitude is if it has to get accomplished, get it accomplished

and they're not adverse to bundling up their sleeves and getting their arms dirty.

Do you base your life-style on your revenue?

Entrepreneurs will seek to develop their business, enlarge their line of products and broaden their services when money setbacks happen. They don't let themselves get to be or remain a victim of fiscal conditions.

If a money setback happens, do you shrink your budget to accommodate the reduction in revenue?

Entrepreneurs send out the payments for themselves first. They center on bringing in the money that supports the life-style they want and invest the rest into their business. That stated, they're likewise cognizant of and accept the fleeting sacrifices that may need to be made in order to achieve a goal.

Do you constantly seek outside advice to make even daily decisions?

Entrepreneurs handle their time and take responsibility for their actions. While they might seek out mentors to guide them to expanded growth, they're in control of their day-to-day actions and don't need somebody else to tell them what to accomplish or prompt them to accomplish it.

Let's look at some more differences

Monday mentality

- Employees fear Monday. (Or, whatever the beginning day of their work week is.)

- Entrepreneurs are not bolted into a work week. They approach each day as a different chance to go after their dreams.

It's not my problem mentality

- Employees have this mentality they view everything on the job by whether or not it's their problem.

- Entrepreneurs view everything as their duty as they have ownership of what is happening in their business.

T. G. I. F. (Thank Goodness It's Friday) mentality

- Employees are constantly looking forward to their off days.

- Entrepreneurs are forever seeking ways to extend their business even when they're not "working" they're considering ways to extend their entrepreneurial talents. They look forward to each day!

When am I going to receive a raise? mentality

- Employees think that raises ought to come according to the calendar, instead of according to their work.

- Entrepreneurs seldom consider when they'll receive an increase. They realize that the more they work towards helping other people the greater their reward will be.

Oh no, what now mentality

- Employees set about meetings with an "oh no" mentality.

- Entrepreneurs set about meetings with a mastermind mentality. They realize that excellent ideas come out of these meetings.

There are a lot more mindsets that we may compare. As a matter of fact if a few have come to mind for you as you read this write them down.

Perusing The Dream Synopsis

There are a lot of employees who are longing to be their own boss, yet are fearsome of what the future may hold if they were business owners. I would like to advise that if you're among those individuals, you'd do well to become a great employee first! I spent a lot of years as an employee and was constantly found to be a model employee.

My entrepreneur bosses constantly gave me high evaluations. In going over the list of employee mentalities, I can frankly tell you that I didn't have those mentalities. I was a great employee!

If you have a want to be on your own one day, going after your dreams as an entrepreneur, you are able to begin now. Approach your occupation as though you owned the company where you work.

Bearing that ownership spirit will reward you on the job and ready you for the day when you are able to pursue your own business. You are able to be an entrepreneur while you're still working. Having this spirit will excite you to go after your own endeavors when you're not on your employer's time clock.

Positive Mindset and Productivity

You spend about a one-third of your life at work. If you're spending it with negative individuals, it may really affect you and bring you down.

By arresting negative thoughts as they enter your ears and not letting them go forward in your thoughts, you'll be doing a lot of the work to remain positive in a negative situation and build your business skills. Here are ways to keep horrible situations at work from bogging you down.

HOW TO BUILD YOUR OWN CASH FLOW EMPIRE. ENJOYING MULTIPLE RESIDUAL AND PASSIVE INCOME STREAM

Possess a life outside your job.

Keep acquaintances who have a good grasp of reality and with whom you are able to share life that's totally unrelated to the job you do. Refuse to even discuss your work outside work hours, particularly if the environment is toxic except when it comes to the ideas for your own business.

Recognize that most of what goes on at work and most of the negativism, even that directed at you, isn't about you.

Think about the stress your colleagues are facing at work, at home and in their personal lives and comprehend that they're projecting and displacing their angriness onto you and other people around them as well. Remember that dealing with people is crucial to being an entrepreneur.

Refuse to let your colleagues' workaholic, ambitions and selfish conduct seep into your system.

It's simple to start letting negative conduct creep in by agreeing with perspectives or taking sides. Rather, choose to rise above it all by staying neutral.

Defend your thoughts; they sooner or later become your reality.

Make certain the negativism around you doesn't continue playing in your head. Play music at your desk at a reasonable volume if you think it helps center you. Take breaks to collect your thoughts. Keep favorable reminders in quotes and pictures around your workspace about what you are trying to learn and accomplish.

Truly think about your options for beginning your entrepreneur journey.

A few bosses may be emotionally abusive; if the company surroundings don't look likely to change, evaluate whether this is truly the best place for you and ways you can start your own thing soon.

You spend eight plus hours a day at your desk juggling calls, emails and correspondences. All the same the stack of paper on your cluttered up desk continues growing taller, you eat more meals at the office than you do at home and you're still hardly meeting your deadlines.

Discover ways to keep away from time traps and to improve existing procedures to be not only more productive at work, but much less stressed and to develop skills that you can use in your own business.

Notice time wasters.

Standard culprits are instant messaging, net surfing, personal calls and gossip with colleagues. The minutes spent on these misdirections may become hours of lost time and lost productivity. Determine limits on these actions and discover ways to politely end conversations.

Confine distractions and interruptions.

Schedule times to follow-up and respond to mail, e-mail and voice mail. If conceivable, switch off instant messenger programs and don't answer personal calls while you work at other tasks.

Coordinate and prioritize.

HOW TO BUILD YOUR OWN CASH FLOW EMPIRE. ENJOYING MULTIPLE RESIDUAL AND PASSIVE INCOME STREAM

If you're constantly searching for items on your cluttered up desk, allow time to organize files, tools and equipment. Keep paper and electronic files in marked folders. On your PC, produce shortcuts and favorites to help find items rapidly and easily.

Utilize a single portable calendar to track all meetings, dates and deadlines.

Produce a schedule to begin and finish a given task and stick to it. Start and finish tasks on time. A daily or weekly "To Do" list may likewise be a helpful tool to stay on track and remain productive.

Be truthful with yourself about your fortes and failings and then budget time and jobs accordingly. It may be helpful to do the things

that you like the least first, as they might be more time consuming and you're more likely to finish more interesting activities.

Compose agendas for meetings and remain inside the allotted time.

Inefficient meetings that go late are a huge cause of productivity loss. Put down all key information like date, time, attendees, schedule items and action items when taking notes. This might save considerable guessing later. When in doubt, document.

Learn to utilize new and better tools to accomplish your work and invest a little time in learning to utilize existing tools more efficiently.

Discover a coach or mentor or take a class in time management, organizational strategies and productive business communication.

Take breaks.

This might seem conflicting when you are swamped. All the same, "crunch time" is when it's even more crucial to stay clear and centered. It's easy to make errors and when feeling deluged. Actually schedule breaks into your day if essential. Even a short walk around the building may clear your head and bring down stress, which promotes productivity.

Learn To Listen to Customers Synopsis

Watch and learn from your people you work with because they frequently demonstrate the habits you'll need to have when you're living the life of an entrepreneur like how to listen to customers.

Notice What People Want

There's a lot of discussion about listening these days. Listening is among the most crucial skills that you are able to learn. If you are able to really stop and listen to your customers, you are able to pave the path to ongoing business success.

Listening calls for paying attention and reacting to the needs and wants of customers. If you want to have your own business, you have to practice the art of active listening.

It is not good enough to react to clients. You have to be able to anticipate their needs. Listening to clients is about placing your company to be the answer to buyer needs, ideally previously them even asking.

Listening is likewise about getting involved with your clients. This

HOW TO BUILD YOUR OWN CASH FLOW EMPIRE. ENJOYING MULTIPLE RESIDUAL AND PASSIVE INCOME STREAM

includes really spending time with them, exploring things that are significant to them, studying magazines and books that are written for them, and being an authority in the things that matter to them.

You're business ought to have an ideal customer. This is the prototype of the perfect client for you. You need to draw in this sort of client, and the more of your clients that fit the ideal, the better. So, it adds up that this is the sort of client you ought to be paying attention to.

A client is somebody who's purchased from you or the company you work for, but it's likewise somebody who may purchase from you. You ought to treat clients, prospects, and general public with equal respect. All the same, you ought to spend your time listening to the individuals who you most want as clients.

Listening may (and ought to) occur everyplace. That being stated, you are able to hone your listening by utilizing particular tools and strategies.

Offline, you ought to be conducting client surveys and just be getting out and talking to clients and people. Go to trade shows and conferences that are likewise attended by your ideal clients. If there are none in your area, begin one.

As your expertness grows, you might want to think about doing a few speaking engagements. This is an awesome way to meet people and to get individuals to tell you about the problems that they face.

Online, the openings are endless. You are able to listen on Twitter with the help of Twitter Search. You are able to track keywords and phrases across the net utilizing Google Alerts.

Forums are a great place to listen. You are able to likewise produce your own listening posts with a blog or podcast. Sure, this is about you talking, but it will likewise force you to explore and learn about your clients. And you are able to encourage dialog and reader comments.

Make sure to listen where clients are talking. If you will be able to find out where ideal clients congregate, online and offline, then you have to be there too.

Active listening will help you to better comprehend and connect with your clients. It will make sales and marketing easier, as you'll be able to position yourself right between the client and the need.

Becoming a great listener will likewise endear you to the individuals you wish to reach. Everybody loves being listened to. So close that trap, put away that profit and loss sheet for a minute, and begin exploring the world of your clients.

Be A Good Provider
Synopsis

We all supply value in the workplace—either by the work we inject as an employee, or with the products and services we sell in our business.

HOW TO BUILD YOUR OWN CASH FLOW EMPIRE. ENJOYING MULTIPLE RESIDUAL AND PASSIVE INCOME STREAM

A great performance review might not be enough to guarantee a promotion or even to keep your line of work. In addition to that, a high-quality product or service might not be enough on its own.

Give First Mentality

Value is in the eye of the observer (think about how much more you may pay for an umbrella on a showery day). Workers who are simple to get along with and reliable with assignments will be more useful to their manager than somebody who produces stress in team meetings and on a regular basis misses deadlines.

In addition to that, a product will be more useful to a consumer if his or her favorite famous person endorses it, if it's on sale, or if it includes a contributed bonus.

At the same time, we're becoming desensitized to ads; we've gotten to be wary of bonus offers, upsells and add-ons. We're seeking authenticity; that's what we value today.

Given the expanded rivalry in the job market, workers have to establish their value to the company in order to get and keep their lines of work, as well as to move ahead to higher positions and acquire customers when it comes to having the entrepreneur mindset.

A lot of consumers are feeling whipped and worried and are guarding their buys cautiously. On the other hand, we're in the middle of a virtual flood of sales offers (no deficit there).

Consumers are picking out the products and service they perceive to be the most useful. You absolutely have to maximize the sensed value of what you offer. But you likewise need to support yourself and your loved ones. So what do you do?

Seek things you are able to add on to your products and services that won't cost you a great deal but are still really useful, e.g., a downloadable e-book or accompanying CD.

Approach somebody who has a complimentary business that services your market, and ask him or her to chip in an additional product or service. It's a win-win, as they acquire the exposure to your clients or customers and you get the extra value for your offer.

Add to the sensed value of your product or service by including case studies and/or recommendations. Think about who may have the peak level of "societal capital" for your audience.

Typically this will be somebody whom your leads may relate to as having like challenges and conditions OR somebody they look up to for having accomplished what they're attempting to accomplish.

Once you consider ways to amp up the sensed value of what you provide, put yourself in your customer's shoes. Is there something about your product or service that you brush aside, but that other people find useful? If you're not certain, survey satisfied buyers and customers.

Workers and business owners, make yourself essential to your team by demonstrating yourself as a connector. Listen for matters that individuals require and match them with individuals, products or services that have them.

Naturally, do this for work projects and additional office tasks, but likewise extend it to personal issues.

For instance, if somebody tells you about an awesome holiday spot, and somebody else is planning their next trip, suggest that the 2 individuals chat about it.

Point out the added value you're already giving to your customers. Maybe you regularly catch clues that everybody else misses. Don't simply assume your clients will notice: point them out in an email or blog post.

In this crowded market, competitive business market and challenging economy, there are chances for the cream to rise to the top. Make certain you remind individuals of your value; why you're the cream as an entrepreneur.

Find A Mentor And Coaching Synopsis

A mentor is an individual with more experience in business, or merely in life, who may help an entrepreneur hone her or his powers and advise him or her on piloting fresh challenges.

A mentor may be a boon to an entrepreneur in a broad array of scenarios, whether they supply pointers on business technique, bolster your networking crusades or act as confidantes when your work-life balance becomes out of whack. However the first thing you need to know when seeking out a mentor is what you're seeking from the arrangement.

What having a personal trainer is to your body, having a coach may be to your mind. Utilizing a coach appears to be the latest way for some individuals to get ahead in today's gaga business world.

Learn From Others

What may your mentor do for you? Ascertaining what type of resource you require is an imperative first step in the mentor hunt. Beginning with a list is a good opening. You might want somebody who's a great listener, somebody socially connected, somebody with expertise in, suppose, marketing, person accessible.

Ideally you may find a mentor with all of these characters, but the reality is you might have to make a few compromises. After you count the characters you're looking for in a mentor, split up that list into wants and needs.

The following step is to "do an informational interview with many candidates and then go back to your standards that way you don't get blown away by chemistry and you remain centered on your business or personal reasons for needing a mentor. By judging a combination of the qualitative and quantitative properties of each of your likely mentors, a prime candidate will come forth.

Bear in mind that it might be advantageous to have more than one mentor. If you think that you might monopolize too much of your mentor's time then several mentors might be the answer.

The benefits of having multiple mentors is that you are able to get a lot of assorted viewpoints and when you have many mentors at a time, if they're

HOW TO BUILD YOUR OWN CASH FLOW EMPIRE. ENJOYING MULTIPLE RESIDUAL AND PASSIVE INCOME STREAM

seated around a table, the synergy between the mentors truly helps move your thinking along.

How to discover a mentor:

Begin with loved ones and friends - When seeking a mentor, begin close to home. Really close to home. Occasionally you are able to talk to your own relatives or friends, individuals who you trust, who you know, who you are able to sit and say 'gee, what do you feel about this?

Think about those in your broadened network - If your friends and loved ones provide you enough unsought advice already, and you don't believe that's the route for you, your left over options are individuals who don't know you as well or don't know you in the least yet.

How do you ask for such a huge commitment from a virtual stranger? The opening move is to get hold of your network of contacts. A positive word from a common acquaintance may go a long way toward getting a mentoring relationship off to a great start.

Additionally, you shouldn't pick out a mentor overnight, which implies you ought to keep your antenna poised to pick up on likely mentors at conferences, trade shows, and so forth. Meeting with a future mentor in person helps construct a rapport and you may wish to wait till that connection develops before tossing out the question.

Think about total strangers - perhaps none of the individuals in your network seem like a great fit for you. Begin doing a little research. Profiles of business owners in magazines and papers may key you in to somebody who equals your style. But when you have a few prospects go forward delicately.

Discover as much as you are able to about the likely mentor and attempt to schedule a brief interview by telephone saying you have a few particular questions or simply generally wish to pick their brain.

You ought to travel to them and, particularly at first, make it as simple for them to help you as you are able to. At the end of your beginning interview, if it appears to have gone well, you may broach the idea of speaking once again, whether by telephone or in person, sometime in the time to come.

Over time, if they feel receptive, you may bring up the idea of a more conventional mentoring relationship with more particular parameters and goals.

Think about the rivalry - Well, not your direct rivalry. For instance, if you're in retail selling windsocks, somebody selling kites isn't in direct rivalry with you but may still have a few insights into the outdoor product industry.

If you have a brick and mortar store, you may even call somebody who does precisely what you do in a far away location, suppose you're in New York City and they're in Arizona.

However the web is increasingly placing retailers even on different continents in rivalry, so step lightly. A different hint would be to seek out counsel from somebody at a business larger than yours who may be less likely to view you as rivalry.

Tap your field - your suppliers, your local chamber of commerce, and relevant trade publishings are great sources for likely mentors. These are all great places to come by knowledgeable individuals, but how do you find somebody who matches your personal flair? Look for a mentor the same way that individuals seek medical professionals, seek recommendations.

Pay for mentoring - But what if you have an awesome idea that you wish to get off the ground rapidly, and you need a fast jolt of expertise? Great informal mentorships are cultivated bit by bit and may frequently last for years. If what you require is a crash program, it may be time to bring in the consultants.

Individuals at all stages of professional evolution need coaches to help them. CEO's often utilize coaches to bounce ideas around, entrepreneurs utilize their coach to help them think strategically about the business, and coaches help other people sort out career decisions.

Think about the effect you are able to have by offering to coach your partners, employees and customers. You are able to be a coach to the individuals around you and help them to accomplish their goals faster and simpler.

Individuals seek coaches for 2 basic causes:

• A few individuals look for coaches to help them discover a balance between their personal and professional lives.

• Other people want coaches to help them get more productive in their business or help step-up their business.

Individuals aren't looking for speedy answers any longer. They're seeking ways to produce lasting change. The traditional consultant doesn't truly bring about lasting change. A coach is a sort of consultant who works with customers to come up with their own changes that are lasting.

Coaching is the next evolutionary stage of consulting. Coaching is a blend of business, finance, psychology, philosophy, transformation and spirituality. It helps individuals get more of what they wish out of life, whether it's business success, fiscal independence, academic excellence, personal success, physical wellness, relationships or career planning.

Coaches are soundboards, support systems, cheerleaders and teammates all rolled into one. Bottom line; the job of a coach is helping other people realize their total potential.
Coaches utilize questioning skills, listening and motivational strategies to help individuals build the skills, knowledge and confidence required to better their professional and personal lives.

A coach is a collaborative partner who helps you achieve things. Coaching isn't a replacement for personal responsibility and personal alteration or choice.

You require a coach if:

• Your business isn't performing as well as you wish. • You feel you're working harder and are less gratified. • Your business is doing well and you're getting sick of working so hard. • A big downsizing in your company is causing big change in the work surroundings.

You think your career is approaching a plateau. • You got a subpar performance review. • You're not able to mold and lead your staff. • You're not easy making strategic conclusions.

A coach supplies you with a place to get a little perspective. A coach is somebody who isn't caught up in all the daily stuff and who may see the big picture.

HOW TO BUILD YOUR OWN CASH FLOW EMPIRE. ENJOYING MULTIPLE RESIDUAL AND PASSIVE INCOME STREAM

Once I decided to follow up on my entrepreneurial urges the conversion from employee to entrepreneur was easier because I initially developed the entrepreneur spirit while working and utilized the time to keep an eye on situations and formulate the skills I would need in order to be successful.

You are able to transition to an entrepreneur mentality too and I trust you will.

5 CHAPTER

Build Your Own Cash Pipeline "Foolproof Strategies on How to Succeed in Network Marketing

The majority of professionals that enjoy this type of income belong to the creative fields such as actors, writers, singers, and inventors.
Unfortunately, not many of us are blessed with the talents Michael Jackson has, let alone the opportunities to be in the lucrative industries. However, there is one budding opportunity for any ordinary individual today to enjoy residual income today in the 21st century.
You've guessed it: it's none other than Network Marketing.

Network Marketing Reviewed
The field of Network Marketing or Multi-level Marketing (MLM) has also been instrumental over the past 60 years or so to make the recurring income concept very popular and attractive.
Here, you can build a network of distributors, referred to as your down line, and generate income outside of your own immediate effort. Working for Network Marketing company is one of the most feasible places where you can generate residual wealth, and so we will now take a look at the secrets to being a successful network marketer.
Choosing a Network Marketing Company
According to a respected journalist, Richard Poe, in his book Wave 4 – Network Marketing in the 21st Century, Network Marketing is responsible for moving over a whopping **$100 billion** of goods and services yearly on the global front. It is therefore very likely that you have already come in contact with some type of Network Marketing product or service. The concept of

HOW TO BUILD YOUR OWN CASH FLOW EMPIRE. ENJOYING MULTIPLE RESIDUAL AND PASSIVE INCOME STREAM

moving goods through an army of independent distributors has earned its place in the marketing world despite the negative publicity suffered by the industry. Network Marketing is here to stay; the question that remains is, "How do I choose a company?"

Here are some very important pointers that would guide you in the right direction. Any company that you can find passing these criteria will be a great company to line up with.

1. A company that has been in business for at least 5 years and has great financial backing, excellent management and a 'distributor first' philosophy. The company should also have a long-term development goal and not just be out for the quick cash.

This may be a pretty tall order to reach but considering that the great majority of start-up Network Marketing companies fail within their first three years you don't want your income stream to suddenly dry up! It's no picnic to discover that after you've spent time, effort and money to build a

solid organization the company closes down because one of those essential elements was missing.

There is the prevalent myth that the best time to join a company is at startup—the so called 'ground floor opportunity'—, but if the truth be told, the ground often caves in leaving many people very unhappy. This does not mean that you should wait for five years to see if a company would do well, because logically, this would mean that no Network Marketing company will ever get started. The point here is that you should assess your risk and know that the chance of losing your money is higher with a new company than with a company having a proven track record.

You know the saying that the proof of the pudding is in the eating; just so the proof of the stability of a Network Marketing company is in the duration of survival. In fact, in over 60 years of Network Marketing history and after tens of thousands of Network Marketing start up companies, only around 42 companies have made it to their 5th birthday.

Any business owner would admit that the first years are the toughest. This is the period when the company is just establishing a footing and income is most likely low. If the company does not have the proper financial backing it is not likely to survive these years. You would not want to join a company that is depending too much on the distributors for survival. A Network Marketing company takes time to build momentum by the very nature of the business - word of mouth advertising, people telling people. Before it reaches top momentum it must have the financial backing to survive the early hurdles. Customer support for the distributors is also a critical part of the company. If their distributors feel neglected then they will simply not stick around. Especially in today's market where there are thousands of Network Marketing companies beckoning. The distributors are the consumers and salespeople, and to neglect them is to commit certain suicide.

A sad reality of the Network Marketing industry is that there are many scam artists that come along just for the quick cash just before they close shop and disappear. This would require that you do your due diligence such as checking consumer alert websites as FTC.gov and WorldWideScam.com among others. These scam artists will normally emphasize the compensation plan over the actual product—if there really

is a product—and apply high pressure sales tactics to persuade you to join the "ground-floor opportunity". These criminals prey on human greed and have little sympathy for the naïve.

2. High quality (unique if possible), reasonably priced products or services that should be, ideally, consumable so users will have to buy over and over again.

Traditionally, Network Marketing companies are able to produce higher quality products simply because they don't have to pay outrageous prices for advertisement. Just think about the millions of dollar paid per year by companies such as Nike to sports stars for a 30 second commercial. This money, if Nike followed the Network Marketing model, could go into developing better quality products and paying their workers better salaries. Because a large part of a normal company's budget goes towards advertising, Network Marketing companies will deliver a higher quality product, all things being equal, per dollar spent.

Also remember that you want to be paid continually so you need a product or service that is consumable so the customer has to keep refilling his supply. Nutritional and telecommunication companies fit this requirement very well. Apart from being consumable, another important factor is how 'needed' this product or service is. The negative side of pushing nutritional products is that most people are only concerned about their health after it is already failing! (You'll do well recruiting at the local hospital). If you are marketing a service such as web hosting, medical coverage or legal services you are more likely to have less attrition in your down line.

If the company is selling a product that you can pick up at your local department store, then you're not likely to do very well. A unique or proprietary product will do better since you'll have less competition—you learn very early that there is no such thing as zero competition although some companies will want to make this claim.

The "acid test" question to apply to the price of the product or service is, "Would I purchase at this price if there wasn't a compensation plan attached to it?" If your answer is "No," then you are looking at a potential pyramid scheme where a product is just attached to the compensation plan to make the opportunity appear legitimate. In these cases you will always find that the compensation plan becomes the selling point and the product or service rarely mentioned.

Here is an informational article on the subject of recognizing and avoiding such schemes: http://www.ftc.gov/bcp/conline/pubs/invest/NetworkMarketing.htm

3. A Compensation Plan that is fair to both full-time and part-time distributors alike with leadership bonuses for those who build large and productive teams. We have already mentioned that a successful Network Marketing company will have a "distributor first" philosophy. In no other place should this be exhibited more than in the compensation plan. It takes only some simple arithmetic to see how many sales or distributors you need in your organization in order to be in profit. Most people don't take the time to do the math and sometimes are "deceived" by the fancy potential income charts that are put out by the company.

The point here is that you need to read between the lines and the fine print to be sure what you are paid for your effort. Most people will skim this section because it may read like a tax code and who likes to do their taxes? That's why we hire accountants.

Compensation plans fall into basically four types:

(a) The Breakaway Plan. This is the oldest and most traditional plan and allows distributors to build and be paid on an unlimited number of front line associates. When the front line associates reach a certain predetermined volume they can "break away" from their up line and form their own organization. In this break away plan the leaders are paid on all their front line and also certain levels down in their break away groups. In this model if you don't work you don't eat. You have to recruit in order to be compensated.

(b) The Multiplan. Here you are only paid on a certain number of levels determined by the company. In this case there are no 'break away' groups. The larger your front line the larger will be your total group size. The lower levels would therefore be much larger than the upper ones. Again if you don't recruit you don't get a check.

(c) The Matrix Plan. In this plan you are limited to the number of recruits you could have on your front line. So in a 3 X 5 matrix you'll have 3 on your front line then 9 on the second level, then 27 on the next and so on. Compared to the two other plans we've looked at the matrix plan limits your success to a certain level. What's so appealing about this plan though is that recruits are told they only need to get 3 and are even promised "spillover" from a "heavy hitter" in their up line. The results are that everyone joins looking for spillover and never makes any personal effort. Results? Certain failure. A matrix, though limited, can work but the distributors must depend on their personal efforts and allow the spillover (if any) to be just an added bonus. One prime example is SOLOBIS.

(d) The Binary Plan. This plan is a special case of the matrix where you can only have two on your frontline, hence 'binary'. The only caveat here is that many such plans require you to balance both sides of your organization before you can get paid. This is really a trick so that the company can keep your money as long as possible and sometimes forever. Some dishonest companies will start off by opening only one side of the binary— called a 'power leg'—as there is no possibility of you getting paid until the other side is opened. By the time the other side is opened many people may have left the company leaving their commission checks behind as well. You are forever left, not only with recruiting, but trying to balance the sides of your team. Beware of such plans!

There are variations of these plans that have come along such as the straight-line plan where you are paid on every one that comes in after you. Companies that follow these plans don't seem to survive very long since most people just join and stand by waiting on their checks. There is no real incentive to work the plan.

Warning: You should always be particularly suspicious of compensation plans that pay out over 60%. This normally means that the product is overpriced, qualification quotas or volumes are almost unreachable or the breakaway structure can rob you of your investment and hard work. If the company uses the breakaway plan you may find your down line disappearing just as you are about to hit the big numbers. If a company intends to be deceptive it will be in the compensation plan; so study it well!

4. Training and solid up line support for your team.

Many companies provide training and promotional materials for their distributors but it is often difficult to strike a balance between product promotion and distributor training. And distributor training normally takes a backseat. You should be wary of companies that charge exorbitant prices for their promotional materials. You are investing your advertising dollars so the company should not seek to make a profit from you here—although many do. You should seek to align yourself with an experienced leader and learn as much as possible from his or her recruiting methods. Be sure to investigate your up line because that can be the one factor that determines success or failure for you. Study the company literature to see who the 'big hitters' are and join their group. It is said that misery loves company; so does success.

5. A wide and even global market if possible.

You may find a company with all the great characteristics that we have looked at so far and then discover that it is not available in your area— ouch! With the advent of the Internet you find that many more companies are going global. This means that your market reach will be wider and chances of building a solid team greatly improved.

Apart from the sheer geography of the company's market reach, is the potential customer base as well. For example, many American nutritional companies are aiming for the 'baby boomers' who are now in their midlife years and make up a good percentage of the buying public—in means and numbers. This demographic of customers want to look younger and are very health conscious. Any product that caters to their needs will most likely have a ready market.

Another big "bubble" when looking at population demographics is the children of the baby boomers. Look at what they are spending money on!

Choosing a company that has a product or service for which there is no ready market will make it very difficult on the distributor. And in this industry one needs a lot of encouragement.

HOW TO BUILD YOUR OWN CASH FLOW EMPIRE. ENJOYING MULTIPLE RESIDUAL AND PASSIVE INCOME STREAM

Network Marketer's Survival Guide

In the Network Marketing industry attrition rate can run as high as over 70%. This means that the majority of people who try a Network Marketing company don't survive the first few months! The upside of this is that 9 out of 10 of those who survive through ten years become very wealthy. This industry has produced more self-made millionaires than any other single industry in America. What a recommendation for Network Marketing!
So if this industry has produced so many self-made millionaires, how is it that more people aren't staying for the long haul? First we would look at some of the major reasons for failure and then some tips to help you escape these traps.
5 Main Reasons Network Marketers Fail
Human beings are complex creatures and so it is always a little risky to make general statements. Over time, however, a pattern emerges and we can get a very good idea why so many people start this business and then drop out.
1. Mishandling of rejection from close family members and their warm market. When someone is first introduced to the concept of Network Marketing they become very motivated—mainly by the income possibilities—to start recruiting right away. Most companies will teach you to start with a list of your warm market and work from there. Even though this is a logical route, rejection from this group can be very discouraging and most people stop there. This means that the majority of recruits will give up after speaking with their spouses for example.
Only lately has Network Marketing become recognized as a viable and respected profession and many are still quick to cry, "Oh! You mean a pyramid scheme". This comes because of the negative press that many

famous companies have received and the general misunderstanding of the public.

2. False expectations for too early results with too little effort.

Depending on the way in which the business is presented, one can get the impression that there is not much effort involved. I mean, just get two who gets two and you can become rich. When early recruits realize that considerable networking and marketing is involved in Network Marketing, disappointment quickly sets in. There is work involved, and any business that presents a plan to you and says that you don't have to do anything is peddling a lie. All successful network marketers worked for their success.

Many marketers do not factor into their planning the cost of advertising their business. This cost can eat up a good chunk of your investment especially when you are just launching. The idea here is that you have to regard this as a normal business and not just a trial run venture.

3. Lack of focus.

Network marketers have gained a reputation of jumping around and changing companies like they change clothing. At least this applies to those who flirt with success but never reach it.

As I mentioned before, those who survive the early years normally go on to do very well. However, there are many people who are looking for the 'next big thing' and keep jumping from opportunity to opportunity. This normally describes the behavior of those in search of the ever evasive 'ground-floor opportunity'. The rule of thumb here is that you should establish yourself in one solid company before venturing off into other companies. And if you do work more than one opportunity, make them complementary to each other. A perfect example is working a leads company which you'll need anyway to feed your primary Network Marketing company. In fact, if you find any tools that enhances your business, why not purchase from a company that has a compensation plan attached?

4. Failure to work an easy to duplicate recruiting plan.

With the advent of the Internet and all the new communication means that it affords, Network Marketing has come a long way from the home meetings and house to house presentations. Doing these presentations was very intimidating to many people and so the recruiting chain often broke along the way. The key here is that if the recruiting machine does not have a system that anyone can comfortably do, it will come to a screeching halt. Good trainers know that a simple system must be in place or the trainer's efforts will not be properly duplicated. If the impression is given that a recruit must be turned into an instant public speaker, giving motivational speeches at the local Hilton, they can be easily scared off.

At the same time, you must take the time to learn the system and become familiar enough with the products that you can tell a friend about its benefit. As a user yourself, this should not be difficult. A caution here is to work the system that has been field tested, rather than trying to invent your own methods. This doesn't mean that you shouldn't be innovative, but there is no use to reinvent the wheel either, so be teachable.

5. Baby-sitting of down line members.

Teaching is surely a part of the game of building a strong team. Some marketers make the mistake of doing too much for their down line members thinking that if they didn't their recruits will leave. This often backfires, however, because the down line members become comfortable and depend too heavily on their up line and never grow strong enough to build their own teams. There is only so much you can do for someone and no more. These spoiled over-dependent down line members can become a liability instead of an asset to your team. So avoid the temptation to micromanage your team; you'll get burnt out. Teach your team members to fish instead of fishing for them.

Secrets of the "Heavy Hitters"

Now we come to the positive side of the equation. Ninety percent of conquering a problem is to identify the problem. Even addicts have to first agree that they have a problem before they can be helped. So if we can quickly review the major reasons why people fail we can just avoid those pitfalls. Let us take a look at these pointers:

1. Be prepared to handle rejection. Who said that any kind of selling was easy? But it all comes down to attitude. If you can understand that a rejection of the opportunity that you are so excited about is not a rejection of you as a person, then you are on your way. "No" must be interpreted as "next". This is easier said than done but it's the price of success. The Internet and other new technologies now allow some rejection proof approaches, such as using lead capture pages and autoresponder messages. These methods serve to "pre-qualify" your prospects. There still must come a time when you will have to be in personal contact with your down line members however.

Part of preparing your mind for these 'negative' people is to fill your mind with positive messages. There are many Network Marketing and "positive thinking" speakers that will help you keep your spirits up. You will be surprised to discover the boost that motivational tapes and books can give to your attitude in general. This is one of the benefits of being in this industry—it teaches you to have a brighter outlook on life.

2. Be realistic in your expectations. To expect too much too soon will only set you up for a possible let down. Accept that this is a legitimate business that requires investment of time and effort and you must be prepared to sow the seeds for the harvest you expect to reap. Who builds a house without first considering the cost?

When you are quoted the salaries of the big recruiters, be sure to ask how much time and money they spent to get to that level. This information will give you a clearer picture.

3. Once you find a reputable company be prepared to stay for the long haul. This goes without saying but if you expect to succeed you must stay the course. The most successful people in life have gone through very trying times but they stuck with it and left a legacy behind. It is often said that tough times don't last but tough people do. The same is true for those seeking to build a solid recurring income. You should commit yourself to at least 3 years before making a decision either way.

Jumping from one opportunity to the next only shows a lack of decision and stability in you planning. Teenagers are expected to fall in and out of love every few months, but married couples have committed for life. Be prepared for a marriage not a fling!

4. Do not make the business more complicated than it needs to be. Stick with what works.

There is always the temptation to improve on the methods that experienced net workers have shown to work. Go with what works, not with what should work. If you find a system that has been working just plug into it and squeeze the last drop of success you can get from this. This means that you must show yourself teachable to your up line and be willing to teach your down line members the same system. Success normally comes from doing what works over and over again until it becomes second nature.

Another note of caution is that you should not expect from your recruits what you are not doing yourself. There a many net workers who will give advice that they are not willing to follow. In other word they get their team members to "do the dirty work" for them. This practice takes away from the real meaning of duplication—I'm doing the same thing that I'm teaching you to do.

5. Train and then let loose!

The real power of Network Marketing is the power of leverage. Rather than using 100% of your own effort, you are using 1% of the effort of a hundred. If your down line members become too dependent upon you then they will be using 110% of your effort. This can easily lead to rapid burnout.

So the key here is to train your front line members, then train them to train their frontline members. As you gain leadership experience in the business then you can occasionally pick up the slack for a colleague. The important thing here is that your team members understand that effort is required on their part or they cannot expect your support.

Here are some additional insider tips on really hitting the ground running. These 'secrets' are learned from the study of those who have made millions in this industry.

6. Talk to many at the same time instead of one at a time.

We just mentioned that the real power of Network Marketing is leveraging your efforts. Did you ever notice that the real successful people in this industry never talk to one person at a time? Just think about it. Your recruiting message or script will be the same for each prospect. You are introducing them to a business opportunity. If you were to use the telephone to do your presentations, how many prospects can you talk to in one day? So here is what the serious marketers do:

(a) Set up a toll free number with a recorded message and invite callers to leave their number and other contact information.

(b) Advertise conference calls where many people can join and listen to your presentation at the same time.

(c) Run a message board on your website where people can ask questions and discuss the business.

(d) Host an online conference chat room.

(e) Buy leads and load them into an autoresponder with your prospecting message. Be careful of here to avoid SPAM complaints. Also confirm that the auto responder company that you use allows you to use purchased leads.

2. Target other network marketers.

This may seem to go against the issue of not jumping from opportunity to opportunity, but it is much easier to work with someone who has already worked in the industry than a totally new person. There are list brokers who specialize in mailing list of distributors from companies that have closed down. For these individuals you don't have to teach them to fish, they already know, and that can be a plus.

In addition to this, you can expect that if they join forces with you they can bring their entire down line from the old company. Of course, one

challenge is that these seasoned marketers will also be more difficult to recruit since they will take a more critical stance of your opportunity.

3. Target business-minded people and entrepreneurs.

HOW TO BUILD YOUR OWN CASH FLOW EMPIRE. ENJOYING MULTIPLE RESIDUAL AND PASSIVE INCOME STREAM

Here again you are targeting people who are already motivated and understand what it takes to run a successful business. These individuals would also already be networking in their businesses and therefore would be in a position of influence. Such people include chiropractors, real estate agents, sales people and Internet marketers. These professionals come in contact with a large number of people and could be the boost that the organization needs. The more 'business minded' your prospects are the more likely you will recruit them.

4. Make a written plan with all your goals and steps to get there.
Psychologists tell us that when we write something down we are more likely to commit to it. That's why you are required in a contract to place your signature on the dotted line—helps you keep your end of the bargain.
Every business owner should have a goal to which they are aspiring. If you aim for nothing you are likely to strike it. If your plan is to get to a recurring income of $10,000 per month then you should set smaller goals on your way there. Say, $3,000 per month after the first year, then $7,000 per month after the second year and finally $10,000 per month by the third year.
A very important part of writing out this plan is to calculate what is required to get to your goal. So if you must call 20 people to get 1 'yes', and that prospect is worth $50 per month to you, you will know how many calls you have to make per month to get to $3,000 per month in one year. Looks simple, but most people don't do this kind of calculation and so they run their businesses with blind expectations.
Knowing where you are going is one of the easiest ways to get there!

5. Continually work to improve your people skills, especially your listening skills.

At its core, Network Marketing is really people management. If you don't like dealing with people then this is not for you. You are always going to be in direct or indirect contact with people and so you should brush up on your people skills.

One of those skills that you'll need to primarily focus on is your listening skills. One of the most common downfalls of Network Marketing is that they talk too much and don't listen enough. This applies to the majority of salespersons. You have to always take time to listen to the customer because if you do - they will tell you what they are looking for! Here are some quick tips to improve your listening skills (particularly on the telephone):

(a) Well ... just stop talking and listen. That's the toughest part.
(b) Learn to view things from the prospect's position. Is your prospect a single mom struggling to make ends meet? Empathize and provide the solution.
(c) Restate what the person tells you to be sure that you understand what they are saying. This also makes the other person feel "heard."
(d) Try not to interrupt them while they are talking—another hard one.
(e) Ask a lot of questions for clarification but not to be confrontational.
(f) Avoid jumping to unnecessary conclusions and learn to "listen between the lines."
(g) Smile! You'll be surprised to see what this does to your tone of voice.

6. Stay informed in what's happening in the industry by subscribing to at least one professional Network Marketing journal.

There are many magazines to choose from and many books written on the subject of Network Marketing. As an "expert" in the field you should be able to speak of it in a professional way and be aware of the latest trends and technologies available to you. Think of how impressed your prospects will be when you can quote them the latest statistics. This helps you to

build immediate credibility with your prospects. If you expect to make $20,000 per month, think about what other professionals with similar salaries had to endure before they reached that level, a doctor for example—years of medical schools, educational loans and internships! Don't be skimpy on your education.

7. Write your own book or produce Network Marketing tapes and CD's.

This may appear to be a tall order but it is not as difficult as it first appears. First you can publish an Ebook even if you have this book written by a professional ghostwriter. You can place a bid at a website such as Elance.com and have writers bid on your job. This book will have your name on the cover and no one has to know that you never wrote one word!

Audiotapes and CD's can be produced at home using a stereo recorder or in a local sound studio. You can also use your computer with the appropriate software and hardware to do this. There are many companies that will reproduce these recordings for you at minimum cost. Having your name on these products can be a real income booster. People want to know that they are following a leader and that is the way you are presenting yourself.

About Affiliate Marketing

Affiliate marketing has been made very popular on the Internet by companies such as Amazon.com, ComissionJunction.com and ClickBank.com.

Strictly speaking, because you are getting a one-time commission for most of your sales in an affiliate program this income is not really recurring. The trick here is to join affiliate programs that offer a monthly service such as a web hosting, or membership websites. Remember the key is that the product should be consumable or requires renewal. Also affiliate or associate programs don't normally pay you beyond the second level so you cannot really build large organizations as in a Network Marketing company, therefore your income is a bit restricted. In this case you will have to spread wide—create a large frontline.

Most affiliate programs don't require you to train or support your customers, so this all balances out. In life it's hard to break the "you get what you pay for" rule. It's the sowing / reaping principle.

In Closing

You should take a look at your income sources and evaluate them to see how many are recurring and how many are linear. The key here is that you may want to "balance your portfolio" so you can have income coming in even if for some reason you are not able to work. Especially as a small business owner this can be critical to your survival.

Even one of your fat monthly checks tucked away on a fixed deposit account will provide you with recurring income—accrued interest.

How long do you think it will take Bill Gates, One of the richest man in the world, to make his first billion if all his bank accounts were presently frozen and taken away? That's the power of residual income.

6 CHAPTER

The Expert Guide to Affiliate Marketing

Being in the affiliate marketing business is not that hard now with the Internet at your disposal. It is much easier now compared to the days when people have to make use of the telephones and other mediums of information just to get the latest updates on the way their program is coming along.

So with technology at hand, and assuming that the affiliate is working from home, a day in his or her life would sound something like this…

Upon waking up and after having breakfast, the computer is turned on to check out new developments in the network. As far as the marketer is concerned there might be new things to update and statistics to keep track on.

The site design has to be revised. The marketer knows that a well-designed site can increase sign ups from visitors. It can also help in the affiliate's conversion rates.

That done, it is time to submit the affiliate program to directories that lists affiliate programs. These directories are means to attract people in joining your affiliate program. A sure way of promoting the affiliate program!

Time to track down the sales you are getting from your affiliates fairly and accurately. There are phone orders and mails to track down. See if they are new clients checking the products out. Noting down the contact information that might be a viable source in the future.

There are lots of resources to sort out. Ads, banners, button ads and sample recommendations to give out because the marketer knows that this is one way of ensuring more sales. Best to stay visible and accessible too.

The affiliate marketer remembered that there are questions to answer from the visitors. This has to be done quickly. Nothing can turn off a customer than an unanswered email.

To prove that the affiliate is working effectively and efficiently, inquiries would have to be paid more attention on. Nobody wants to be ignored and customers are not always the most patient of all people. Quick answer that should appear professional yet friendly too.

Hot Tip Affiliate products that are limited in availability will always increase sales.

Super Affiliates Know Their Products

Now that you know how you are going to be handling the people side of marketing and you know a lot more about your intended niche than the AVERAGE affiliate, it's time to research some products. You already know from your people research (forums, surveys, etc.) that a lot of people in the niche are having a certain problem…let's say putting in golf.

Now that you know you're looking for a "putt straightener" product, it's a simple matter to do some sea r ch i ng to find products that will help people pu t t
 straighter. Here's how to do that effectively and as quickly as possible.

There are a TON of websites that you can use to find applicable products, but the top 4 to use are: http://www.associateprograms.com/directory/ http://www.affiliateprograms.com   http://www.commissionjunction.com/ http://www.clickbank.com/marketplace.html

Individual products may have an affiliate program of it's own so if you personally use a program check out selling it to others. Check your favorite products to see if they have an affiliate program and you can pick up extra income by just telling people what you are personally using and giving them a chance to have the same great experience!

Join This Affiliate Program For Generous Recurring Commissions http://www.Espired.com/Affiliates.html

If you do not use the product yourself here's where you have to do some digging. Once you've found a list of products that you may want to sell to your new niche, you need to explore those products thoroughly. Check out the sales page you'll be sending your visitors to; check out the company behind the product…are there any complaints about them on the Internet? Are the affiliates happy with them? Check out the terms of service for affiliates…how often do they pay you…how do they pay you…is there a minimum commission…so there are no surprises for you when you start to sell a bunch of their products.

Get in contact with their affiliate manager, if they have one, or the product owner and see what tools they have to help you sell their product. See what type of support you feel you'll get from them.

In the process of doing all the necessities, the marketer is logged on to a chat room where he or she interacts with other affiliates and those under that same program. This is where they can discuss things on how to best promote their products.

There are things to be learned and it is a continuous process. Sharing tips and advices is a good way of showing support. There may be others out there wanting to join and may be enticed by the discussion that is going on. There is no harm in assuming what opportunities ahead.

The newsletters and Ezines were updated days ago, so it is time for the affiliate marketer to see if there are some new things happening in the market. This will be written about in the marketer's publication to be distributed to the old and new customers.

These same publications are also an important tool in keeping up to date with the newly introduced products. The marketer has put up a sale and promotion that customers may want to know about. Besides, they have to keep up with the deadline of these sales written in the publications.

It is that time to show some appreciation to those who have helped the marketer in the promotions and sale increase. Nothing like mentioning the persons, their sites and the process they have done that made everything worked.

Of course, this will be published in the newsletters. Among the more important information that have been written already.

The marketer still has time to write out recommendations to those who want credible sources for the products being promoted. There is also time to post some comments on how to be a successful affiliate marketer on a site where there are lots of wannabes.

Two objectives done at the same time. The marketer gets to promote the product as well as the program they are in. Who knows, someone may be inclined to join.

Time flies. Missed lunch but is quite contented with the tasks done. Bed time....

Ok, so this may not be all done in a day. But then, this gives you an idea of how an affiliate marketer, a dedicated one that is, spends the marketing day.

Is that success looming in the distance or what?

The 3 Things All Affiliate Marketers Need To Survive Online

Now every affiliate marketer is always looking for the successful market that gives the biggest paycheck. Sometimes they think it is a magic formula that is readily available for them. Actually, it is more complicated than that. It is just good marketing practices that have been proven over years of hard work and dedication.

There are tactics that have worked before with online marketing and is continuing to work in the online affiliate marketing world of today. With these top three marketing tips, you will be able to able to increase your sales and survive in the affiliate marketing online.

What are these three tactics?

1. Using unique web pages to promote each separate product you are marketing.

Do not lump all of it together just to save some money on web hosting. It is best to have a site focusing on each and every product and nothing more.

Always include product reviews on the website so visitors will have an initial understanding on what the product can do to those who buys them. Also include testimonials from users who have already tried the product. Be sure that these customers are more than willing to allow you to use their names and photos on the site of the specific product you are marketing.

You can also write articles highlighting the uses of the product and include them on the website as an additional page. Make the pages attractive compelling and include calls to act on the information. Each headline should attract the readers to try and read more, even contact you. Highlight your special points. This will help your readers to learn what the page is about and will want to find out more.

2. Offer free reports to your readers.

If possible position them at the very top side of your page so it they simply cannot be missed. Try to create autoresponder messages that will be mailed to those who input their personal information into your sign up box. According to research, a sale is closed usually on the seventh contact with a prospect.

Only two things can possibly happen with the web page alone: closed sale or the prospect leaving the page and never return again. By placing useful information into their inboxes at certain specified period, you will remind them of the product they thought they want later and will find out that the sale is closed. Be sure that the content is directed toward specific reasons to buy the product. Do not make it sound like a sales pitch.

Focus on important points like how your product can make life and things easier and more enjoyable. Include compelling subject lines in the email. As much as possible, avoid using the word "free" because there are still older spam filters that dumps those kind of contents into the junk before even anyone reading them first. Convince those who signed up for your free reports that they will be missing something big if they do not avail of your products and services.

3. Get the kind of traffic that is targeted to your product.

Just think, if the person who visited your website has no interest whatsoever in what you are offering, they will be among those who move on and never come back. Write articles for publication in e-zines and e-reports. This way you can locate publications that is focusing on your target customers and what you have put up might just grab their interest.

Try to write a minimum of 2 articles per week, with at least 300-600 words in length. By continuously writing and maintaining these articles you can generate as many as 100 targeted readers to your site in a day.

Always remember that only 1 out of 100 people are likely to buy your product or get your services. If you can generate as much as 1,000 targeted hits for your website in a day, that means you can made 10 sales based on the average statistic.

The tactics given above does not really sound very difficult to do, if you think about it. It just requires a little time and an action plan on your part.

Try to use these tips for several affiliate marketing programs. You can end maintaining a good source of income and surviving in this business that not all marketers can do.

Besides, think of the huge paychecks you will be receiving!

How To Become A Super Affiliate In Niche Markets

Over the past years, web hosting has grown bigger than it used to be. With more companies getting into this business and finding the many benefits it can give them, the demand for web hosting has never been higher. These seem to be the trend of today.

The possibility of quality web hosting companies separating themselves from the rest of the industry is anticipated. If this is done, the unprofessional and incompetent ones will suffer.

Support will be the number one consideration for people when choosing a web host. It will be obvious that traditional advertising will become less and less effective. Most people would rather opt for the web host based on things that they see and hear. Also based on the recommendations by those who have tried them and have proved to be a successful.

This is a great opportunity for web hosting affiliates and resellers alike. There would hundreds of web hosting and programs to choose from that the difficulty in finding the right one for them is not a problem anymore.

How does one become a successful affiliate in the niche markets using web hosting?

If you think about it, everyone who needs a website needs a web hosting company to host it for them. As of now, there is really no leading hosting industry so most people choose hosts based from recommendations. Usually, they get it from the ones that have already availed of a web hosting services.

With the many hosts offering affiliate programs, there is the tendency to find the one which you think will work best for you. Think of the product you will be promoting. Pattern them to the site and see if they are catering to the same things as you are.

When you have been with one host for quite some time and seem not to be making much despite all your effort, leave that one and look for another. There is no use in trying to stick to one when you would be before off in another one. Things will only have to get better from there because you already have been in worst situations.

Try this out. If you are quite happy and satisfied with your web host, try to see if they are offering an affiliate program you can participate on. Instead of you paying them, why not make it the other way around; them paying you. The process can be as easy as putting a small "powered by" or "hosted by" link at the bottom of your page and you are already in an affiliate business.

Why choose paying for your for your web hosting when you do not have to? Try to get paid by letting people know you like your web host.

Always remember that when choosing a web host, choose the one that is known for its fantastic customer support. There are also many hosting affiliate programs. Residual affiliate program is also being hosted. This is the program wherein you get paid a percentage every month for a client that you refer. This can allow you to have a steady source of income. With perseverance, you can even be quite successful in this field.

There are a lot of niche markets out there just waiting for the right affiliate to penetrate to them and make that dollars dream come true. Knowing which one to get into is being confident enough of your potentials and the good results you will be getting.

Web hosting is just one affiliate market you could try out and make some good and continuous income. Just remember that to be successful on your endeavor also means that time, effort and patience is needed.

Nobody has invented the perfect affiliate market yet. But some people do know how to make it big in this kind of market. It is just knowing your kind of market and making the earnings there.

So Many Affiliate Programs! Which One Do I Choose?

Ask questions first before you join an affiliate program. Do a little research about the choices of program that you intend to join into. Get some answers because they will be the deciding point of what you will be achieving later on.

Will it cost you anything to join? Most affiliate programs being offered today are absolutely free of charge. So why settle for those that charge you some dollars before joining.

When do they issue the commission checks? Every program is different. Some issue their checks once a month, every quarter, etc. Select the one that is suited to your payment time choice. Many affiliate programs are setting a minimum earned commission amount that an affiliate must meet or exceed in order for their checks to be issued.

What is the hit per sale ratio? This is the average number of hits to a banner or text link it takes to generate a sale based on all affiliate statistics. This factor is extremely important because this will tell you how much traffic you must generate before you can earn a commission from the sale.

How are referrals from an affiliate's site tracked and for how long do they remain in the system? You need to be confident on the program enough to track those people you refer from your site. This is the only way that you can credit for a sale. The period of time that those people stay in the system is also important. This is because some visitors do not buy initially but may want to return later to make the purchase. Know if you will still get credit for the sale if it is done some months from a certain day.

What are the kinds of affiliate stats available? Your choice of affiliate program should be capable of offering detailed stats. They should be available online anytime you decide to check them out. Constantly checking your

individual stats is important to know how many impressions, hits and sales are already generated from your site. Impressions are the number of times the banner or text link was viewed by a visitor of your site. A hit is the one clicking on the banner or text links.

Does the affiliate program also pay for the hits and impressions besides the commissions on sales? It is important that impressions and hits are also paid, as this will add to the earnings you get from the sales commission. This is especially important if the program you are in offers low sales to be able to hit ratio.

Who is the online retailer? Find out who you are doing business with to know if it is really a solid company. Know the products they are selling and the average amount they are achieving. The more you know about the retailer offering you the affiliate program, the easier it will be for you to know if that program is really for you and your site.

Is the affiliate a one tier or two tier program? A single tier program pays you only for the business you yourself have generated. A two tier program pays you for the business, plus it also pays you a commission on the on the sales generated by any affiliate you sponsor in your program. Some two-tier programs are even paying small fees on each new affiliate you sponsor. More like a recruitment fee.

Lastly, what is the amount of commission paid? 20% - 80% (and some cases, 100%!) is the commission paid by most programs. .01% - .05% is the amount paid for each hit. If you find a program that also pays for impressions, the amount paid is not much at all. As you can see from the figures, you will now understand why the average sales amount and hit to sale ratio is important.

These are just some of the questions that needed answering first before you enter into an affiliate program. You should be familiar with the many important aspects that your chosen program should have before incorporating them into your website. Try to ask your affiliate program choices these questions. These can help you select the right program for you site from among the many available.

Which Affiliate Networks To Look Out For When Promoting

There are many horror stories about affiliate programs and networks. People have heard them over and over again, that some are even wary of joining one. The stories they may have heard are those related to illegal programs or pyramid schemes. Basically, this kind of market does not have real, worthy product.

You do not want to be associated with these schemes. It is obvious you want to be with a program that offers high quality product that you will readily endorse. The growing number of those who have joined already and are succeeding immensely is proof enough that there are reliable and quality affiliate programs out there.

Why participate in an affiliate program?

It allows you to work part-time. It gives you the opportunity to build a generous residual income. And it makes you an owner of a small business. Affiliate programs have already created lots of millionaires. They are the living testimony of how hard work; continuous prospecting, motivating and training others pay off.

If ever you are deciding to join one, you must take note that you are getting into something that is patterned to what you are capable of. This will be an assurance that you are capable of doing anything to come out successful.

How do you choose a good affiliate program to promote? Here are some tips you may want to look over before choosing one:

1. A program that you like and have interest in.

One of the best ways of knowing if that is the kind of program you wish to promote is if you are interested in purchasing the product yourself. If that is the case, chances are, there are many others who are also interested in the same program and products.

2. Look for a program that is of high quality.

For instance, look for one that is associated with many experts in that particular industry. This way, you are assured that of the standard of the program you will be joining into.

3. Join in the ones that offer real and viable products.

How do you know this? Do some initial research. If possible, track down some of the members and customers to give you testimonial on the credibility of the program.

4. The program that is catering to a growing target market.

This will ensure you that there will be more and continuous demands for your referrals. Make inquiries. There are forums and discussions you can participate in to get good and reliable feedbacks.

5. A program with a compensation plan that pays out a residual income and a payout of 40% or more would be a great choice.

There are some programs offering this kind of compensation. Look closely for one. Do not waste your time with programs that do not reward substantially for your efforts.

6. Be aware of the minimum quotas that you must fulfill or sales target that is too hard to achieve.

Some affiliate programs imposes prerequisites before you get your commissions. Just be sure that you are capable of attaining their requirements.

7. Select one that has plenty of tools and resources that can help you grow the business in the shortest possible time.

Not all affiliate programs have these capacities. Make use you decide on one with lots of helpful tools you can use.

8. Check out if the program has a proven system that can allow you to check your networks and compensation.

Also check if they have it available online for you to check anytime and anywhere.

9. The program that is offering strong incentives for members to renew their membership each time.

The affiliate program that provides continuous help and upgrades for its products have the tendency to retain its members. These things can assure the growth of your networks.

10. Be aware of the things that members are not happy about in a program.

Like with the ones mentioned above, you can do your checking at discussion forums. If you know someone in that same program, there is no harm asking if there are many downsides involved.

Have a thorough and intensive knowledge about the affiliate program and network you will be promoting on.

Knowing the kind of program you are getting yourself into will make you anticipate and prevent any future problems you may encounter.

Easy Profits Using PPC In Your Affiliate Marketing Business

PPC or Pay-Per-Click in full is one of the four basic types of Search Engines. PPC is also one of the most cost-effective ways of targeted Internet advertising. PPC or Pay Per Click, can accounts to 8 billion dollars a year or more

Let us take a quick look at how PPC Search Engines work.

HOW TO BUILD YOUR OWN CASH FLOW EMPIRE. ENJOYING MULTIPLE RESIDUAL AND PASSIVE INCOME STREAM

These engines create listings and rate them based on a bid amount the website owner is willing to pay for each click from that search engine. Advertisers bid against each other to receive higher ranking for a specific keyword or phrase.

The highest bidder for a certain keyword or phrase will then have the site ranked as number 1 in the PPC Search Engines followed by the second and third highest bidder, up to the last number that have placed a bid on the same keyword or phrase. Your ads then will appear prominently on the results pages based on the dollar amount bid you will agree to pay per click.

How do you make money by using PPC into your affiliate marketing business?

Most affiliate programs only pay when a sale is made or a lead delivered after a visitor has click through your site. Your earnings will not always be the same as they will be dependent on the web site content and the traffic market.

The reason why you should incorporate PPC into your affiliate marketing program is that earnings are easier to make than in any other kind of affiliate program not using PPC. This way, you will be making profit based from the click throughs that your visitor will make on the advertiser's site. Unlike some programs, you are not paid per sale or action.

PPC can be very resourceful of your website. With PPC Search Engines incorporated into your affiliate program, you will be able to profit from the visitor's who are not interested in your products or services. The same ones who leave your site and never comes back.

You will not only get commissions not only from those who are just searching the web and finding the products and services that they wanted but you will be able to build your site's recognition as a valuable resource. The visitors who have found what they needed from you site are likely to come back and review what you are offering more closely. Then they will eventually come back to search the web for other products.

This kind of affiliate program is also an easy way for you to generate some more additional revenues. For example, when a visitor on your site does a search in the PPC Search Engine and clicks on the advertiser bided listings, the advertisers' account will then be deducted because of that click. With this, you will be compensated 30% to 80% of the advertisers' bid amount.

PPC is not only a source of generating easy profits; it can also help you promote your own site. Most of the programs allow the commissions received to be spent for advertising with them instantly and with no minimum earning requirement. This is one of the more effective ways to exchange your raw visitors for targeted surfers who has more tendencies to purchase your products and services.

What will happen if you when you integrate PPC into your affiliate program?

PPC usually have ready-to-use affiliate tools that can be easily integrated into your website. The most common tools are search boxes, banners, text links and some 404-error pages. Most search engines utilize custom solutions and can

provide you with a white-label affiliate program. This enables you, using only a few lines of code, to integrate remotely-hosted co-branded search engine into your website.

HOW TO BUILD YOUR OWN CASH FLOW EMPIRE. ENJOYING MULTIPLE RESIDUAL AND PASSIVE INCOME STREAM

The key benefits? Not only more money generated but also some extra money on the side. Plus a lifetime commissions once you have referred some webmaster friends to the engine.

Think about it. Where can you get all these benefits while already generating some income for your site? Knowing some of the more useful tools you can use for your affiliate program is not a waste of time. They are rather a means of earning within an earning.

Best know more about how you can use PPC search engines into your affiliate program than miss out on a great opportunity to earn more profits.

Using Product Recommendations To Increase Your Bottom Line

In affiliate marketing, there are many ways in which you can increase your earnings and maintain the account that you have worked so hard for already. Most of the techniques and tactics can be learned easily. No need to go anywhere and any further. They are available online, 24 hours a day and 7 days a week.

One of the more important ways of increasing affiliate marketing bottom line and sale is through the use of product recommendations. Many marketers know that this is one of the most effective ways in promoting a certain product.

If the customers or visitors trust you enough, then they will definitely trust your recommendations. Be very careful in using this approach, though. If you start promoting everything by recommendation, your credibility will actually wear thin. This is seen especially when recommendations are seemingly exaggerated and without much merit.

Do not be afraid to mention things that you do not like about a given product or service. Rather than lose any points for you, this will make your recommendation more realistic and will tend to increase your credibility.

Furthermore, if your visitors are really interested in what you are offering, they will be more than delighted to learn what is good about the product, what is not so good, and how the product will benefit them.

When you are recommending a certain product, there are some things to remember on how to make it work effectively and for your advantage. Sound like the true and leading expert in your field.

Remember this simple equation: Price resistance diminishes in direct proportion to trust. If your visitors feel and believe that you are an expert in your niche, they are more inclined to making that purchase. On the other hand, if you are not exuding any confidence and self-assurance in endorsing your products, they will probably feel that same way and will go in search of another product or service which is more believable.

How do you establish this aura of expertise? By offering unique and new solutions they would not get anywhere else. Show proof that what you are promoting works as promised. Display prominent testimonials and endorsements from respected and known personalities, in related fields of course.

HOW TO BUILD YOUR OWN CASH FLOW EMPIRE. ENJOYING MULTIPLE RESIDUAL AND PASSIVE INCOME STREAM

Avoid hype at all costs. It is better to sound low key and confident, than to scream and seek attention. Besides, you would not want to sound unprofessional and have that thinking stick to your potential customers and clients, now would you? Best to appear cool and self-assured at the same time.

And remember; prospects are not stupid. They are actually turning to experts and may already know the things that you know. If you backup your claims with hard facts and data, they would gladly put down hundreds, or even thousands worth of money to your promotions. But if you don't, they are smart enough to try and look at your competitors and what they are offering.

While recommending a product, it is also important that you give out promotional freebies. People are already familiar with the concept of offering freebies to promoting your own products. But very few people do this to promote affiliate products. Try to offer freebies that can promote or even have some information about your products or services.

Before you add recommendations to you product, it is given that you should try and test the product and support. Do not run the risk of promoting junk products

and services. Just think how long it took you to build credibility and trust among your visitors. All that will take to destroy it is one big mistake on your part.

If possible, have recommendations of products that you have 100% confidence in. Test the product support before you begin to ensure that the people you are referring it to would not be left high and dry when a problem suddenly arouse.

Have a look at your affiliate market and look at the strategies you are using. You may not be focusing on the recommendations that your products need to have. You plan of action is sometimes not the only thing that is making your program works.

Try product recommendation and be among those few who have proven its worth.

Using Camtasia to Increase Your Affiliate Checks

Since there are already lots of people getting into affiliate marketing, it is no wonder that the competition is getting stiff. The challenge is to try and outdo other affiliates and think of ways to be able to attain this.

There are also many tips and techniques being taught to these affiliate in order to best plan their strategy for their program to work effectively so that more earnings will be achieved.

What better way to wow your prospects and customers than to record and publish top notch, full motion and streaming screen-captured videos. Nothing like feeling your hard work getting paid by having your customers jumping up excitedly in great anticipation to buy your product right there and then.

This is Camtasia in action. It is a proven fact; giving your customers something they can actually see can explode your online sales instantly.

You do not need to have trainings and education to be able to know how this system can work for your affiliate program. Anyone can create stunning videos, from multimedia tutorials and step-by-step presentations available online. The process is like having your customers seated next to you and looking at your desktop, as you show them the things they need to see and hear. All this done step by step.

For those who does not know it yet, how does Camtasia works?

1. It can record your desktop activity in a single click. No need to have to save and compile all your files because it is recorded right there and then.

2. Can easily convert your videos into web pages. Once converted you can have your customers visiting that certain page. Videos are easier to understand and take in unlike reading texts which oftentimes is a trying thing to do.

3. Upload your pages. Publish them through blogs, RSS feed and podcasts. You may want your Camtasia videos to get around and reach out to other people that may be potential customers in the future. Nothing like being visible in many sites and pages to advertise yourself and get your message through.

There are other things you can do with your affiliate program using Camtasia. You can…

Create stunning multimedia presentations that are proven to increase sales because all the senses are engaged. This also has the tendency to reduce skepticism among hard-to-please customers.

Reduce refunds and other customer issues by demonstrating visually how to use your product and how to do it properly. Complaints will also be minimized because all the facts and the presentation are there for the customers to just see and hear about.

Promote affiliate products and services using visual presentations. This is an effective way of redirecting your viewers straight to your affiliate website after they are finished with the video. Make the most of the presentation by putting your site location in the end and make them go there directly if they want more information.

Multiple your online auction bids exponentially when you give your readers a feel of what you have to offer. Based from reports, auctions that includes pictures increases bidding percentage by 400%. Imagine how much higher it will be if it were videos.

Publish valuable infoproducts that you can sell for a much higher price. It will be all worth the price because of the full colored graphics menu and templates that you will be using.

Minimize miscommunication with your customers. Instantly showing them what you want they wanted in the first place is making them understand clearly the essence of your affiliate program. The good thing about multimedia is, nothing much can go wrong. It is there already.

These are just some of the things you can do with Camtasia that can be very helpful in your chosen affiliate program.

Note that the main purpose of using Camtasia is to boost the income that is generated from your affiliate program. Although it can be used for entertainment and enjoyment purposes, which is not really a valid reason why you choose to get all through that trouble.

Try to focus on the goal that you have set upon yourself to and achieve that with the use of the things that may be quite a lot of help in increasing your earnings.

Top 3 Ways To Boost Your Affiliate Commissions Overnight

The ideal world of affiliate marketing does not require having your own website, dealing with customers, refunds, product development and maintenance. This is one of the easiest ways of launching into an online business and earning more profits.

Assuming you are already into an affiliate program, what would be the next thing you would want to do? Double, or even triple, your commissions, right? How do you do that?

Here are some powerful tips on how to boost your affiliate program commissions overnight.

1. Know the best program and products to promote.

Obviously, you would want to promote a program that will enable you to achieve the greatest profits in the shortest possible time.

There are several factors to consider in selecting such a program. Choose the ones that have a generous commission structure. Have products that fit in with your target audience. And that has a solid track record of paying their affiliate easily and on time. If you cannot seem to increase your investments, dump that program and keep looking for better ones.

There are thousands of affiliate programs online which gives you the reason to be picky. You may want to select the best to avoid losing your advertising dollars.

Write free reports or short E-Books to distribute from your site. There is a great possibility that you are competing with other affiliates that are promoting the same program. If you start writing short report related to the product you are promoting, you will be able to distinguish yourself from the other affiliates.

In the reports, provide some valuable information for free. If possible, add some recommendations about the products. With EBooks, you get credibility. Customers will see that in you and they will be enticed to try out what you are offering.

2. Collect and save the email addresses of those who download your free E-Books.

It is a known fact that people do not make a purchase on the first solicitation. You may want to send out your message more than six times to make a sale.

This is the simple reason why you should collect the contact information of those who downloaded your reports and E-Books. You can make follow-ups on these contacts to remind them to make a purchase from you.

HOW TO BUILD YOUR OWN CASH FLOW EMPIRE. ENJOYING MULTIPLE RESIDUAL AND PASSIVE INCOME STREAM

Get the contact information of a prospect before sending them to the vendor's website. Keep in mind that you are providing free advertisement for the product owners. You get paid only when you make a sale. If you send prospects directly to the vendors, chances are they would be lost to you forever.

But when you get their names, you can always send other marketing messages to them to be able to earn an ongoing commission instead of a one-time sale only.

Publish an online newsletter or E-zine. It is always best to recommend a product to someone you know than to sell to a stranger. This is the purpose behind publishing your own newsletter. This also allows you to develop a relationship based on trust with your subscribers.

This strategy is a delicate balance between providing useful information with a sales pitch. If you continue to write informative editorials you will be able to build a sense of reciprocity in your readers that may lead them to support you by buying your products.

3. Ask for higher than normal commission from merchants.

If you are already successful with a particular promotion, you should try and approach the merchant and negotiate a percentage commission for your sales.

If the merchant is smart, he or she will likely grant your request rather than lose a valuable asset in you. Keep in mind that you are a zero-risk investment to your merchant; so do not be shy about requesting for addition in your commissions. Just try to be reasonable about it.

Write strong pay Per Click ads. PPC search engine is the most effective means of advertising online. As an affiliate, you can make a small income just by managing PPC campaigns such as Google AdWords and Overture. Then you should try and monitor them to see which ads are more effective and which ones to dispose of.

Try out these strategies and see the difference it can make to your commission checks in the shortest of time.

How To Avoid The 3 Most Common Affiliate Mistakes

As the handbook draws to a near end and closing publication, here are some hazard signs and dangerous waters you shouldn't be treading on in the affiliate marketing scene!

So listen up…

Affiliate marketing is one of the most effective and powerful ways of earning some money online. This program gives everybody a chance to make a profit through the Internet. Since these affiliate marketing programs are easy to join, implement and pays a commission on a regular basis, more an more people are now willing in this business.

However, like all businesses, there are lots of pitfalls in the affiliate marketing business. Committing some of the most common mistakes will cost the marketers a large portion taken from the profit they are making everyday. That is why it is better to avoid them than be regretful in the end.

Mistake number 1: Choosing the wrong affiliate.

Many people want to earn from affiliate marketing as fast as possible. In their rush to be part of one, they tend to choose a bandwagon product. This is the kind of products that the program thinks is "hot". They choose the product that is in demand without actually considering if the product appeals to them. This is not a very wise move obviously.

Instead of jumping on the bandwagon, try to choose a product in which you are truly interested in. For any endeavor to succeed, you should take some time to plan and figure out your actions.

Pick a product that appeals to you. Then do some research about that product to see if they are in demand. Promoting a product you are more passionate about is easier than promoting one for the sake of the earnings only.

Mistake number 2: Joining too many affiliate programs.

Since affiliate programs are very easy to join, you might be tempted to join multiples of affiliate programs to try and maximize the earnings you will be getting. Besides you may think that there is nothing wrong and nothing to lose by being part of many affiliate programs.

True, that is a great way to have multiple sources of income. However, joining multiple programs and attempting to promote them all at the same time will prevent you from concentrating on each one of them.

The result? The maximum potential of your affiliate program is not realized and the income generated will not exactly be as huge as you were thinking initially it would. The best way to get excellent result is by joining just one program that pays a 40% commission at least. Then give it your best effort by promoting your products enthusiastically. As soon as you see that it is already making a reasonable profit, then maybe you can now join another affiliate program.

The technique is to do it slowly but surely. There is really no need to rush into things, especially with affiliate marketing. With the way things are going, the future is looking real bright and it seems affiliate marketing will be staying for a long time too.

Mistake number 3: Not buying the product or using the service.

As an affiliate, you main purpose is to effectively and convincingly promote a product or service and to find customers. For you to achieve this purpose, you must be able to relay to the customers that certain product and service. It is therefore difficult for you to do this when you yourself have not tried these things out. Thus, you will fail to promote and recommend them convincingly. You will also fail to create a desire in your customers to avail any of what you are offering.

Try the product or service personally first before you sign up as an affiliate to see if it is really delivering what it promises. If you have done so, then you are one of the credible and living testaments aware of its advantages and disadvantages. Your customers will then feel the sincerity and truthfulness in you and this will trigger them to try them out for themselves.

Many affiliate marketers make these mistakes and are paying dearly for their actions. To not fall into the same situation they have been in, try to do everything to avoid making the same mistakes.

Time is the key. Take the time to analyze your marketing strategy and check if you are in the right track. If done properly, you will be able to maximize your affiliate marketing program and earn higher profits.

7 CHAPTER

iPhone & iPad App Cash

There are many people who are making millions of dollars with applications for the iPhone and iPad. Fortunately, many iPhone apps will also work for the iPad, so you can kill two birds with one stone.

There is never going to be a better time than now to be an app developer. While the field is constantly becoming more and more competitive, the market is still relatively young. If you get in now, you have a very good chance to make a lot of money. Remember, the pioneers in an industry usually establish dominance right away, so it's important to jump in right now!

In this report, I'm going to teach you some of the basics of creating an iPhone or iPad app. I'll also give you some resources with more advanced information.

The time to do this is NOW! The longer you wait, the more money you are leaving on the table!

Generating App Ideas

Generating an idea for an app will probably be your biggest hurdle, and that can easily be overcome with some creative brainstorming techniques.

Remember, an app doesn't even have to be useful or involved in order to be successful. Have you heard of Joel Comm's app? It's called iFart. Basically, it lets users choose from several different types of farting sounds and play them through their phone. It's useless, but it has been downloaded many, many times. At about 99 cents per download, it has made back his development costs many times over!

Copy Existing Apps

One of the easiest ways to get an idea is simply by looking through popular apps and copying them. Obviously, you wouldn't want to copy their concept exactly. Instead, download the app yourself and try to figure out its major weaknesses.

If possible, look for comments about that app. Find out what people don't like. Then you can create an app that addresses those weaknesses in order to make customers happier with your app than the original!

Some of the world's best products are simply copies of existing products. Today's computers are just copies of the original PC – with significant improvements, of course. There's nothing wrong with taking ideas as long as you make major changes and make the product unique in several ways.

What do YOU Need?

Maybe there's something you wish your own iPhone could do that you haven't seen addressed in an app. This is great, because if you want this, other people probably do, too!

Make a list of some of the things you would love to be able to do with your phone, and then search the App Store to see if an existing app will do it. If not, you might be able to create the first one! If so, you can always copy and improve it!

Outsourcing Development

HOW TO BUILD YOUR OWN CASH FLOW EMPIRE. ENJOYING MULTIPLE RESIDUAL AND PASSIVE INCOME STREAM

You don't have to worry about a lack of programming experience. Even if you have never written a line of code in your life, you can still release successful apps.

The main way to create apps without programming is to outsource the development. If you have a very specific ideas for your app, this may be your only option.

Make sure you hire someone who has significant experience creating iPhone and iPad apps. Many programmers think they know how to create an app, but soon discover it's more complex than they thought. You should be certain to hire someone who has already created apps that work on the iPhone and iPad, and who can show you examples.

Never pay 100% of the development cost up front! Try to pay a 10% to 25% deposit. If the programmer has excellent, verifiable references, you might go as high as 50% up front. You never want to risk paying 100% up front, no matter how impeccable their references are. What if (God forbid) they passed away during development? Anything can happen.

In order to ensure you get the app you really want, be sure you have as many details as possible about the app before you start looking for a programmer. You will want to map out functionality, screen layouts, etc. so the programmer knows exactly what you want before work starts. This will save you both a lot of time, money, and frustration.

Also, be certain to get your programmer to sign an NDA and a NCA. An NDA is a non-disclosure agreement that ensures they won't talk to anyone about your app, potentially opening you up to competition before your app is even available. An NCA is an agreement that the developer won't release an app that competes with yours, and can also prevent them from developing a similar app for someone else for a period of time. An attorney can help you draw up these agreements. You may even want to get an NDA while in the hiring process so you can talk about your app in detail to ensure the programmer is confident they can do what you want before you hire him or her.

Software and Services for Development

If you have an app idea that is very simple, you may be able to use one of the ready-made solutions that are now available to build your app. These programs and services can create very simple apps for as little as $30!

Don't expect to get a custom app that will perform specific functions for this price. But you could, for example, get an app that would deliver news and updates from popular golf blogs and news sites by RSS. Golf fans might be willing to pay 99 cents for an app that would give them the latest news in the world of golfing at their fingertips.

Services include:

http://www.AppIncubator.com

http://www.Kanchoo.com

http://www.MyAppBuilder.com

http://www.BuildAnApp.com

Marketing an App

Many app developers erroneously believe that all they have to do is upload their app to the App Store and sales will magically begin to flood in. This might happen, but it is extremely unlikely. The App Store is becoming more and more competitive all the time, and you must promote your app if you want to ensure significant sales.

There are practically endless ways to promote an app, but I'm going to go over some of the best ways to get an app off the ground quickly.

Forum Marketing

One of the best places to market your app is via forums in your app's niche. If you have a golf app, why not market it through golfing forums?

HOW TO BUILD YOUR OWN CASH FLOW EMPIRE. ENJOYING MULTIPLE RESIDUAL AND PASSIVE INCOME STREAM

You definitely do not want to spam your app. Instead, sign up to the forum and place something like this in your signature file (usually found in your preferences or control panel.)

"Jim Smith – Creator of the Golf News Blast app for iPhone and iPad"
If the forum allows links in signatures, you can also place a link to your app in your signature.
Then all you have to do is post on the forum. Post helpful tips and advice, answer questions, and be friendly. As you become more well-known, more people will notice your signature and word will spread about your app.
Press Releases
A press release is a great way to go, especially if you have an app that is very unique. If you can get picked up by major news outlets, you could get a lot of publicity very quickly!
Blogging
If you have a blog in your app's niche, make sure you post about it regularly. If not, consider commenting on popular posts on other blogs in your niche!
Resources
If you want more in-depth information about making money with iPhone and iPad apps, I highly recommend the following products.
Earn with Apps – This is the quintessential guide to making money with your own iPhone and iPad apps! From A-Z this system will teach you exactly how to get started!
Create Apps with No Experience – If you want to create apps yourself, this is THE guide for you! Learn exactly how to create iPhone and iPad apps without any prior experience or programming knowledge!
How to Market iPhone Apps – Do you need more ideas for marketing your app? This guide will teach you everything you need to know to send your sales through the roof!

What Is Internet Marketing?

Internet marketing is now called so many other names – e-marketing, web marketing, marketing, digital marketing, online marketing and the like. However, in plain and simple language, it can be defined as the marketing of one's products or services that a business or person offers through the use of the internet.

This type of marketing encompasses a very broad area of the subject as it also includes many types of marketing strategies like email and wireless media marketing. Under this general scope of internet marketing also falls the aspects of ECRM or electronic customer relationship management and digital customer data.

Why is internet marketing a big advantage to many businesses?

The world wide web has given us many unique and essential benefits. This technology enabled the entire world to be connected with each other in a matter of seconds. In terms of online businesses, the internet has provided a global portal in which goods and services can be sold and bought by almost anyone and in any part of the world.

With internet marketing, all types of businesses have enjoyed the lower costs of information dissemination and advertisements. The internet's interactive nature has benefited business marketing through instant responses and its ability to elicit them in the

HOW TO BUILD YOUR OWN CASH FLOW EMPIRE. ENJOYING MULTIPLE RESIDUAL AND PASSIVE INCOME STREAM

fastest way possible. Furthermore, internet marketing has tied together all the aspects of creativity, technicality, advertisement, sales and product development.

With its inexpensive cost, internet marketing has also enabled businesses to save on their means of reaching their target market or audience. Through a small fraction of the cost of traditional advertisements, businesses can further allow their customers to conduct research and eventually purchase their products in the most convenient way. This also makes them more appealing to their clients because they can provide results in a very short span of time.

Internet marketing has also allowed these businesses to measure their statistics in a much easier and inexpensive way. Since almost all the aspects of this marketing type can be measured, tested and traced through the use of ad servers, advertisers can easily use and observe their data as to which ads reap the most customer views or purchases. This way, online businesses will be able to determine which of their advertising messages are more appealing to their target customers. The results of all their campaigns can be tracked right away since this marketing initiative simply requires a customer to click the ads, visit a certain website or perform a desired action like filling out a form or purchasing a product or service.

Now as a beginner in the world of internet marketing, you will be responsible for the task of bringing in potential clients by providing them the services or the company that suits their needs or preferences in various internet venues.

You will help these customers find the product that they are looking for. The targets are the people who have computers with internet access. Entrepreneurs like you can visit your online store anytime. Consumers can also do the same whenever they want. The future of the world wide web is so bright with its projected online consumer traffic reaching almost 60% and over 80% of these customers shopping online. So if you are determined to make it successful for you, you may just find yourself enjoying the benefits of having an online business that will give you more profit in the long run.

With that said, internet marketing brings you many advantages of incurring minimal costs in starting up your business including cheaper advertising options, a global marketplace, becoming your own boss, promoting stuff that you are passionate about and profiting from these passions along the way. Sounds amazing doesn't it?

Though there are many benefits from internet marketing, it does come with its own share of risks and investments. You must understand that this process will not let you rake in a lot of cash quickly. Your time, diligence, persistence and passion for learning more are very important in your success in internet marketing.

Those who think that this is a get rich quick scheme are bound to be disappointed. Though many businesses have become extremely successful, you will find that those who have failed in this venture have simply wished to become overnight millionaires. The realities of a physical business are still applicable to your online store, including tax payments, customer services and even hiring employees.

HOW TO BUILD YOUR OWN CASH FLOW EMPIRE. ENJOYING MULTIPLE RESIDUAL AND PASSIVE INCOME STREAM

Furthermore, it is important that you know that starting an online business is not free. There are costs that may be less than what will be used in building a physical business, but you will still have to shell out for web design, software, hosting, domains and advertising costs. Another reality of having an online business is site downtime. Yes, your site may go down due to technical difficulties or glitches, and this will probably bring a lot of frustration not just on your part but also on the customers' end. Every single minute or second that your site is unavailable to visitors and potential customers, you will be losing money. You need to be prepared for this.

Furthermore, you cannot just rely on a certain system and have it run on autopilot to generate profit. Technology changes and the industry evolves rapidly, making any "autopilot system" that is supposed to generate cash a complete lie. A marketing tactic that worked for someone in the past may not work for you at all in the future. Therefore, it is very important to keep yourself updated with new technologies and marketing trends.

Competition will always be around so if you do not keep yourself informed and you do not work hard, you will not stand out in the crowd. You have to make an impact! Work hard because if not, you can be sure that one of your competitors is out there doing so. Besides, if you want your business to be a long-term investment, your first profits should go back to your site's services and advertising efforts. Maximize your profits and do not just cash out your first earnings. It will also be helpful to learn about taxation and other related laws that affect this industry.

This way, you know what your tax and legal advantages are once you set up your business. This will also help in protecting your assets, thus, it should never be overlooked.

With all these realities in mind, you will need to be very determined to stand out in this industry. Internet marketing is not for the person who likes simple routines. You should be flexible in learning new strategies and trends in order to keep up with your competition.

Now that you know what internet marketing is and all the good and bad that comes with it, you will now learn the marketing methods that online businesses have been using in order to promote their services and products to the global marketplace. The following methods that will be discussed further in the next few passages are:

Affiliate marketing Article marketing E-mail marketing Blog marketing Pay per click ads or PPC Search engine optimization or SEO Pop-up ads Banner ads Social media marketing Mobile marketing

These internet marketing methods are not equal at all. Each of them have strategies to reach a target market and will produce varying results based on your goal, marketing pitch and relationship with your customer. Whether you are going to market your own website or choose to get involved in affiliate marketing, you are most likely going to use a couple of these methods at various times. Remember, what you earn in this industry is always proportionate to all the effort and time you have invested in developing your website.

Now let's proceed to the juicy part of this subject. In the next few pages, you will learn each of the internet marketing methods mentioned above. You will get to know what they are, what they do, how they work and why they are effective.

1. Affiliate Marketing

Affiliate marketing is an online practice wherein a business rewards an affiliate for the visitors or customers brought in by his marketing efforts. The rewards are either cash or gifts and are given for either an offer completion or site referral. In this process, there are four players – the merchant, network, publisher and customer. Recently, this market has grown complex with the secondary players like affiliate management agencies, third party vendors (specialized) and super-affiliates. It works by simply using the affiliate's website to drive traffic to the merchant's own site or to allow visitors to be forwarded to the merchant's main web page.

Basically, this is also what we can call revenue sharing between the online merchants and online affiliates. The compensation given to the affiliates depend on how many user clicks, sales or registrations were made on the merchant's website via their own. Affiliate marketing enables the automation of the advertising processes and the payment for desired actions. Merchants have preferred this internet marketing strategy because it is a "pay per performance" model, where they do not incur any expenses for marketing their products unless the affiliate produces the results they need.

Affiliate marketing can also be translated as a type of business relationship where you, as an affiliate, promote a merchant's services which is different from yours. This means that you do not need to have your own product in order to venture into affiliate marketing. You only need to promote your business provider's services and products.

This is how it works – you need to have a web page that contains a link that directs your users or visitors to the main page or online store of the merchant. When one of your site visitors clicks on that link and purchases something from the merchant's website, you will get a sort of commission or a referral fee. This way you are the one driving traffic to your merchant's website through your own web page. The merchant will pay you whenever a visitor from your site buys something or signs up for something on their site. A special affiliate link is assigned to your web page, making it easy for the merchant to track customers coming from your site. One merchant is allowed different affiliate links and all of them will direct the users to its website.

Another strategy that works in affiliate marketing is the use of web page codes or web cookies. This is actually a very interesting way to still profit even if your visitor clicks on the affiliate link and does not purchase from the merchant's site at once. How does this work? The moment a user clicks on the link, a cookie is stored in his computer, indicating that he or she visited the merchant's site and recording your page as the one that referred him to that website. If, let's say a couple of weeks later, the user finally decides to buy something from the merchant's online store and types the web address of the merchant directly into his browser, the cookies stored in his computer will still recognize the purchase as a referral from your affiliate link, allowing you to receive a compensation from the merchant. Note that cookies have expiration, so you must read the affiliate program terms carefully to check the life span of these cookies.

HOW TO BUILD YOUR OWN CASH FLOW EMPIRE. ENJOYING MULTIPLE RESIDUAL AND PASSIVE INCOME STREAM

The success of affiliate marketing has also paved way for the rise of many online companies such as Amazon.com, which now has thousands of affiliates.

2. Article Marketing

Article marketing is an online advertising strategy used by many businesses to market their websites, products or services by writing short articles that are related to their industry. It is the practice of posting these keyword-focused writings on article syndication sites that have a good readership following. These articles will then be distributed and published in the marketplace. Many opine that article marketing is an essential element in any internet marketing strategy. These articles have the intention of providing information and entertainment to online users. Typically these articles have a resource box or bio box that indicates the references and contact information of the writer's business. The resource box may also contain a link back to the website that the author is promoting in order to attract the readers to visit that website.

Articles that are well-researched and written are usually released and distributed for free in order for the business to gain more credibility within the market. Through these articles, a website or online business will be able to attract more new clients. Internet marketers usually submit the articles to several article directories in order to maximize the results of their online campaign. In order to avoid the filtering process of the internet for duplicate content, internet marketers attempt what we call article spinning or article rewriting and rewording to give certain variations to the original article. Through this, the article can acquire site visitors coming from several websites for article directories. Getting your article to be featured in niche blogs or focused content websites that are managed by others is a good and popular strategy in terms of article marketing. If you are a guest blogger on these websites, you will be able to introduce your business to an interested audience that may have been otherwise unreachable.

The common practice in internet publishing is to have your articles use relevant keywords and catchy titles with around 250 to 500 words in the body. If you incorporate the keywords or keyword phrases in your articles, it is possible to get more search engine traffic.

Which, among the hundreds of article directories, should you submit your articles to? This is actually one of the most tedious tasks in this marketing method. Today, businesses and experts usually outsource their article marketing methods including the submission process. The most popular article directories that are recommended include EzineArticles, IdeaMarketers and GoArticles.

Article marketing can also help you generate leads that you can include in your email list. In writing your articles, you must give the readers an offer so irresistible that it will prompt them to visit your website and sign up for your services. Once you have their information, you can start creating a sales-winning partnership with them. Failing to do this will not give you another chance to sell to your leads.

Among the best offers you can give your readers may include quizzes, special reports on a certain topic, free consultation sessions or free book chapters. This way, your readers will be enticed to provide you with their email addresses that you can use to further send marketing news and information about your website.

Overall, the most important factor in article marketing is to get people to visit your website and sign up or purchase one of your services. Writing articles that are accurate, specific and helpful will attract more potential leads or clients.

3. Email Marketing

This is one of the most cost-efficient methods of internet marketing that promotes your business. In order to execute an effective and successful email campaign, you need the right information to achieve your desired results.

Email marketing is a direct marketing method that makes use of emails to communicate a commercial message to your target market. It is the process of sending messages to your previous or current customers in order to encourage them to do business with you again and in turn enhance your business relationship with them. E-mail marketing is also used to acquire new clients and convince your current customers to buy something at once.

There are several advantages in using this type of internet marketing. For one, almost all internet users have email accounts that they check regularly. With this form of communication, advertisers can easily reach those who have signed up to receive regular communications regarding subjects that interests them. It is cost-effective and has a short impact time.

Email marketing can be categorized into three types: direct e-mail, intermediary e-mail and retention e-mail.

Direct e-mail usually is an email message with commercial sales content. They are usually sent to customers who have previously used a certain product or service or to potential clients in your target audience who might enjoy and benefit from the service you are offering. Direct mail marketing may make use of a company's email list or a purchased or shared email list or a list that is acquired from a third party service. These third party services may already know which audience can be target through e-mail marketing or they may conduct an analysis to find out which email addresses will bring the highest conversion or responses for your business.

Retention email or newsletter mail on the other hand, are designed and written for promotional use. They aim to provide a long-term impact to the customer's mind, thus, their content is more than a sales message. The retention mail specifies the benefits of the products or services that a company offers in a more informative format.

Intermediary e-mail is a message sent by a company delegated by the main provider to send out advertising and marketing emails to a list of subscribers that is usually owned by the intermediary company.

In order to be successful in e-mail marketing, you must always use all relevant information that is necessary for your business. You may send messages to your customers if you find that they will benefit from what you are about to offer them. In sending these emails, you must also write an informative and straight forward headline

in order to grab your customer's attention. Before sending out your email, check the message and use both text and HTML formats to make sure that your message will be received and read, or you may include options to view your mail in these formats.

4. Blog Marketing

Blogs have become one of the useful platforms for internet marketing. Subscribers of a blog usually sign up to receive content on a regular basis and since most subscribers remain loyal when they receive relevant and useful information, a strong following and readership will be a good way to reach these potential customers and get them to either sign up or purchase a service from your business. Blogs have continuously reached their targets most of the time, making them a very effective way to market one's services or products.

Blog marketing, as the name suggests, is done via a web blog through a series of weekly or daily posts about a certain topic. A lot of businesses have used blogs to communicate and interact with their customers while featuring their services. Organizations have also used blogs to share and review a product's features and benefits prior to their official launch. They also pave way for companies to gather or receive feedback from the consumers in order to confirm if their services and products meet the expectations of their clients.

Since blog marketing focuses on interaction with online users, you may also start blogging in order to market your product line to get more exposure to the cyber market.

However, you will have to write and design a blog that will stand out from your competitors. This way, your blog will also gain more popularity, making more websites want to link to it. The more websites linking to your blog, the more traffic and profit you will get. You must always remember to give your audience or target subscribers a reason to always visit your blog. If your subscriber leaves any comments, be sure to send them a thank you email. Hold small contests every now and then where you can give away discounts and coupons to your subscribers. You may also ask your followers to post the link of your blog to their own websites in exchange for free product samples.

5. Pay-per-click or PPC

PPC or Pay-per-click advertisements, also known as Cost Per Click, are used to bring in traffic to websites where advertisers provide compensation to the hosting site whenever their ad is clicked. There are two models for determining how much is to be paid per click – flat-rate and bid-based rate. In both models, advertisers consider the value of a click from a certain source where such value depends on the type of customer that the company is targeting and what can be gained from his or her visit (which is usually revenue).

If you currently have a running website or a blog and would like to earn extra profit, you can try this internet marketing method. Put in pay-per-click ads on your blog or web page and merchants will pay you a percentage every time your visitors click on them.

One of the most popular PPC is Google Adsense. It is very easy to add this to your blog and more so if you use Blogger which is also managed by Google. Adsense displays a number of advertisements that target a specific audience on your blog. In order to sign up for pay-per-click ads like Google Adsense, you will need to complete an online form as your official application.

6. Search Engine Optimization (SEO)

Whenever you search for a topic on Google, Yahoo or MSN, you usually get pages and pages of websites that have the keywords you typed in the search bar. Have you ever wondered why a particular website is listed first on the results of your search? The primary reason for this is Search Engine Optimization.

Search engine optimization allows a website to become search engine friendly, making it rank higher on search results compared to other websites that have the same keyword contents. Usually, these search engines read and archive sites regularly so that they can be found easily whenever a search is performed by a user. For example, if a user types in "parenting" in the search bar and your website is about the same topic and is optimized properly, your website will appear in the first page of the search results.

Basically, SEO makes your website easier for these search engines to understand. Its goal is to increase your website's rank in the search results that will in turn bring in more traffic to your site. Remember, the more traffic you get, the more potential for profit you will have.

On-site and off-site factors are the ones that can determine your search engine rankings. On-site factors include your page content and your title heading. Off-site factors like pages that link to your site, words used to link to your page and how long such link has existed also come into play. It is important that you focus on your site's SEO continuously because if you get good search engine rankings consistently, you will always have free traffic.

7. Pop-up Ads

During your internet surfing time, you probably have come across many of these pop-up ads. These are advertisement windows that appear once you visit a website. Their aim is to generate traffic or simple capture your email address.

Many people have found this internet marketing method quite annoying since it disrupts them from getting information from the website they are viewing. However, these ads, intrusive as they have been tagged, also have certain advantages. For one, they are much more effective than banner ads. They pull up a 15% click through rate while the banners only yield a mere 3%. Pop-up ads also are effective and gives a click through percentage of 6.5. Since they are more effective than banner ads, they also cost you a lot more. However, the return on investment with the use of these ads is much higher. Furthermore, when this ad is the only window on the page, there will be no other images that will conflict with the brand that you are selling.

In the recent years though, these advertising methods have become less popular due to the development of pop-up blockers.

8. Banner Ads

A banner ad is basically a graphic, text or an image displayed on websites that aim to promote a company's product or service. They are actually small HTML codes, but their importance in internet marketing and business is significant. Banner ads vary in sizes and orientation but will often come in rectangular shape and are 486 x 60 pixels high (full banner). There is actually no universal rule when it comes to banner ad file sizes, but the size will still depend on the website where it will be displayed. These sites impose certain limits to banner sizes since it adds up to the total size of the web page they are displayed on, thereby resulting to more waiting times while the page loads on a browser.

Due to the banner ads' graphic elements, you may find these ads somehow similar to those you see in printed media such as magazines and newspapers. However, these banner ads have the ability to direct the user to the advertiser's main web page. If you are interested in displaying or posting a banner on a certain website, you can arrange with the publisher to have your banner posted or pay a banner network to post the ad on a number of websites. You may also arrange with the publisher to simply display their ads on your site in exchange for them displaying your banner ads.

9. Social Media Marketing

Social media marketing is basically the process of marketing your business through social media portals such as Facebook, YouTube and Twitter. This allows for businesses to have a more personal and dynamic interaction and connection with their clients and potential customers.

Strategies in social media marketing can be as simple as maintaining a blog, a Facebook or Twitter account or attaching "tweet this" icons to the end of your articles or ads. It can also be as complex as having a full campaign that includes blogging, social networking, tweeting and spreading viral videos.

As marketing is the process of informing consumers what your business is, who you are and what your products are, social media further helps in introducing your business to a global network of possible customers. The use of social media to prove a business' identity and to create business relationships with people who do not have the chance be aware of your products and services is a highly recommended option in internet marketing. Moreover, it is an avenue that can be accessed by anyone who has an internet

connection and is an inexpensive way to implement your marketing strategies and business campaigns.

10. Mobile Marketing

Mobile marketing has been a concept that has attained various definitions. It is primarily described to be the marketing strategy that makes use of mobile media to communicate with a target market. Recently a more updated definition was given by the Mobile Marketing Association, saying that mobile marketing is actually a combination of practices that gives organizations the ability to engage, communicate and interact with their audience through a mobile device or network.

The most popular mobile device used for this is a cell-phone. To use this medium, you will need to set up a short code and have your customers register to receive your SMS or text messages. Mobile optimization will also make sure that your website is displayed correctly on a mobile phone browser. Search engine optimization has undergone many changes that made internet marketers become more interested in the mobile version of their optimized websites compared to the traditional website optimization. Most mobile phones today have internet access or wireless capabilities. These devices have provided more flexibility on both the business' and consumers ends in terms of receiving and sending data related to the products or services which a company offers.

The most typical types of mobile marketing include the use of MMS or Multimedia Messaging Service, Bluetooth technology, Infrared and Mobile Internet. Marketing through a mobile device is now a trend in many developed countries where almost everyone has a mobile phone. This is also a more cost-effective method of promoting your business and is much easier for most age groups to understand. More time is now spent online with the use of these devices, making your business available to consumers who are always on the go and would still want to receive updates from your end.

In MMS mobile marketing, a slideshow of text and images that may include a video or audio is a perfect way to capture a potential customer's attention effectively. The ad is delivered via MMS. The use of Bluetooth technology in marketing makes use of radio based frequencies to transfer data on higher speeds. Infrared, on the other hand, is a bit limited, as its frequency range only reaches as far as 1 meter.

Mobile marketing is a new way to ensure customer awareness and boost your sales. With all the new smart phones, tablets and modern mobile devices, mobile marketing is definitely destined to progress in the years to come.

All the major internet marketing methods have been discussed in detail in this guide. It is now up to you to choose which one you prefer, however, remember the things that you need to have in order to succeed – good research, a positive mindset and attitude, diligence, patience and focus. All the best.

ABOUT THE AUTHOR

APOSTLE OWEN LAWRENCE

Apostle Of Wealth Distribution. A visionary and provocative thinker, Global Business Microfinance Consultant, the CEO of OMBFC, the Founder and Senior Pastor of MZDMC, anointed preacher, calling as an Apostle.mentor, author, professional trainer, entrepreneur, Financial Coach, A global humanitarian doing charitable work to help the needy, A heart of compassion to the hurting, message of freedom and empowerment to the oppressed and disenfranchised. www.owenlawrence.site . olaw2007@yahoo.com

www.ingramcontent.com/pod-product-compliance
Lightning Source LLC
Chambersburg PA
CBHW031920240526
45464CB00021B/619